*Sociology in Social Work*

# LIBRARY OF SOCIAL WORK

GENERAL EDITOR: NOEL TIMMS
Lecturer in Social Science and Administration
London School of Economics

# Sociology in Social Work

*by Peter Leonard*

*Lecturer in the Department of Social Science*
*University of Liverpool*

LONDON

ROUTLEDGE AND KEGAN PAUL

*First published 1966*
*by Routledge and Kegan Paul Ltd*
*Broadway House, 68-74 Carter Lane*
*London, E.C.4*

*Printed in Great Britain*
*by Northumberland Press Limited*
*Gateshead on Tyne*

© *Peter Leonard 1966*

361
L 5 8 1 s

# Contents

19633

## General editor's introduction

The Library of Social Work is designed to meet the needs of students following courses of training for social work. In recent years the number and kinds of training in Britain have increased in an unprecedented way. But there has been no corresponding increase in the supply of text-books to cover the growing differentiation of subject matter or to respond to the growing spirit of enthusiastic but critical enquiry into the range of subjects relevant to social work. The Library will consist of short texts designed to introduce the student to the main features of each topic of enquiry, to the significant theoretical contributions so far made to its understanding, and to some of the outstanding problems. Each volume will suggest ways in which the student might continue his work by further reading.

In their task of understanding human problems, social workers have received valuable help from psychology, particularly from psychoanalysis. They are now beginning to look to sociology for further, sometimes corrective, insight into themselves and their clients and the situations in which they meet. In this volume, Peter Leonard outlines some of the main sociological ideas and theories that might help social workers and usefully discusses some of the difficulties involved in using this source. We should not expect immediate and easy returns, but, as the author indicates, the long-term gains are likely to be considerable.

This volume is one of a number devoted to the exploration of the knowledge social workers use in understanding their clients and the society in which they live. In the past, insufficient attention has been given to the knowledge on which social work is based, to its various sources (different schools of psychology, sociology, social work practice, etc.), to the varying degrees of confidence it should command, and to the difficulties in testing its truth and establishing its relevance to social work. This book offers an introduction to the knowledge to be gained in the study of sociology by social workers.

NOEL TIMMS

# 1

# Sociology and its relation to social work

Social workers have always maintained that they must view their clients with a framework which takes into account the biological, psychological and sociological aspects of man. The professional education of social workers has in recent years emphasised the central importance of the study of 'human growth and behaviour' in which these aspects are examined at every stage of development from birth to death. Social work practice, on the other hand, has placed special emphasis upon psychological understanding, and has tended to neglect sociology as a discipline apparently of less immediate relevance to the task of dealing with the problems of individuals and groups. Psychology, with its focus on the individual, appeared to social workers to have clear therapeutic implications, whereas sociology, with its focus on social interaction, seemed less easy to use. There is no denying that this is the case, and some social work educators have maintained that 'it is only recently that sociological theory has begun to catch up with personality theory in developing material of use to the caseworker' (Hollis, 1959). Others, such as Wooton (1959) have laid the blame entirely upon the social worker's need 'to pose as a miniature psychoanalyst or psychiatrist' and thus neglect the socio-logical dimensions of clients' problems.

In order to understand and evaluate the contribution which may be made by sociology to social work it will be necessary to seek the reason for its relative neglect by social workers in the past. This chapter will examine the interaction (and lack of it) between sociology and social work historically and provide a brief account of the development of sociology in Britain and the United States.

## Definitions and descriptions

We may use the term *social work* to denote the processes used by welfare agencies to help individuals, groups or communities to cope more effectively with their problems of social functioning. Thus, social work consists of social casework (with individuals), social group work (with groups) and community organisation or community development (with communities). Clearly, these divisions are not mutually exclusive, particularly that between group work and casework, but they are necessary for the study of social work methods. In this book most of what is said about social work will, in fact, relate particularly to casework, the most developed and widely used method of social work in Britain, though reference will be made from time to time specifically to group work and com-munity development.

Social work is a professional discipline which has its own body of knowledge based upon practice but scientifi-cally largely unvalidated. It makes use of the results of academic work, such as sociology and psychology, and consequently owes allegiance to certain scientific assump-tions. Yet because social work is a means of implementing society's decisions on the handling of certain forms of behaviour, it is concerned deeply with values and with the use that can be made of knowledge for social action, rather than knowledge for its own sake.

Sociology is the scientific study of the social behaviour of human beings. It is concerned with social interaction: 'Sociology is the science that deals with social groups: their internal forms or modes of organisation, the processes that tend to maintain or change these forms of organisation, and the relations between groups' (Johnson 1961). Whether sociology, like social work, is concerned with the practical applications of knowledge, or whether it is concerned exclusively with the pursuit of knowledge for its own sake is a matter of dispute among sociologists. What is clear, however, is that social problems such as delinquency, disruptive family conflict, and mental illness, have to do with the functioning and malfunctioning of groups, and that scientific knowledge about the processes that maintain or change the organisation of groups, whether they be gangs, families or communities, is of considerable importance in the task of attempting to solve these problems.

As sociology is the study of social interaction within and between groups, it takes for analysis groups of decreasing order of size and complexity from whole societies, through social institutions such as the family, to the social relationships which make up the social institutions. At this final level of social analysis, which covers much of the same area of interest as social psychology, a distinction can nevertheless be made between the sociological approach which is concerned with social interaction itself, and the psychological approach which studies individual behaviour, and which takes into account the *effects* of the interaction of others for the purpose of understanding the *individual*. (See Parsons, 'Psychoanalysis and Social Structure', 1954.)

3

It is possible to list the major areas of sociology which are of particular interest to social work:

1. Sociological theory and scientific methods
2. Culture and its relationship to society and the individual
3. Community social structure, urban and rural
4. Small groups
5. Family and Kinship
6. The study of organisations (including the social services)
7. Social stratification (especially social class)
8. Ethnic groups and cultural conflict
9. Social deviance (crime, suicide, mental illness, etc.) and social control.
10. Social change

In this book we shall be able to refer to a fraction of the sociological knowledge which is of value to social work.

## Social Darwinism and British social work

In Britain, social work as we know it today is usually seen as having its origins in the work of the Charity Organisation Society beginning in the second half of the nineteenth century. It is not without significance that the influence of this Society was high at a time when social thought in Britain was under the dominating influence of Herbert Spencer's theory of evolution. The C.O.S. held strongly to the doctrine of personal inadequacy as the cause of poverty and this coincided with Spencer's Social Darwinism. Spencer is a seminal figure in sociology, and his three volume *Principles of Sociology* (1877) was the first full scale systematic sociological analysis. Spencer's view was that history was a natural process and that the state should not interefere with the resulting natural balance when the individuals who made up society voluntarily

4

respected each others' rights. In particular, Spencer held that the state should not attempt to do things which the free individual could do better for himself. Thus, the state should have no concern with education, economic affairs or any form of social welfare, and socialism should be opposed as tending to strengthen the power of the state. This opposition to social progress and social amelioration by state action is reflected in the *laissez-faire* philosophy which influenced the C.O.S. who wished to help people to adapt to the necessary rigours of economic competition.

The dominance of evolutionary theory in nineteenth-century sociology can be seen in the Social Darwinism of another important early sociologist Gumplowicz (1838-1909), who held the view that the state had nothing to do with justice and that it should make no attempt to further the welfare of its citizens. August Comte (1798-1857), who gave sociology its name and who may be seen as the founder of modern sociology, was also essentially conservative and saw sociology as a bulwark against revolution. His philosophy of Positivism with its view that social phenomena resulted from natural laws was clearly open to conservative interpretation. In the United States, Comte's Positivism was used to defend slavery in the Southern States in two books published in 1854, Henry Hughes' *Treatise in Sociology*, and George Fitzhugh's *Sociology for the South*. Thus, Positivism and Social Darwinism produced a sociology which 'recognised only the universal law of natural development. It therefore traces back the history of society and human civilisation to the constant struggles of social groups against each other. This social struggle is the counterpart to the struggle for existence and the survival of the fittest in nature' (Maus, 1962).

The influence of sociological theory on social work, at the end of the nineteenth century, then, tended to bolster its dogmatic individualism. In the C.O.S. the social workers in the District offices realised the need to 'get to know the district' and were, as Todd (1961) has pointed out, more inclined to reject the doctrine of personal inadequacy as the cause of poverty than the Central Council of the Society which remained rigidly committed to extreme individualism. A striking example of this attitude may be seen in the Society's opposition to the findings of Charles Booth's survey of poverty. Charles Booth (1840-1916) is an important figure in the early development of British sociology, for his *Life and Labour of the People of London* (1889-1903) provided a model for future social surveys in Britain and established the traditional British sociological interest in practical results and social amelioration. Booth's survey showed the statistical relationship between poverty, misery and crime on the one hand, and relative comfort and regular income on the other. Booth described the general conditions under which each class of society lived in London, and was assisted in undertaking the survey by a whole army of voluntary workers, including social workers and school attendance officers. However, his work struck at the whole doctrine of personal inadequacy and the C.O.S. establishment was forced to reject his findings. A C.O.S. report of 1892 remarked: 'We do not share Mr. Booth's natural affection for his table of causes. . . . His mastery over figures is only exceeded by the mastery of figures over his own imagination' (see Todd, 1961).

Charles Booth's concern with social reform has characterised a good deal of British sociology and thus might have influenced social work to a much greater extent but for the ideological objections of the C.O.S. However, some sociologists have themselves objected to the very practical nature of much of British sociology, and Booth's fellow social investigators at the turn of the century, Beatrice Webb and Seebohm Rowntree are not usually described

6

as 'real' sociologists because of their lack of interest in developing sociological theory. Some have held (see Barnes and Becker, 1938) that the development of sociology in Britain as an independent science was hindered because of this intimate association with social reform, which tended to produce a parochialism of outlook.

At this time, however, not all evolutionary sociological theories implied a rigidly individualistic attitude to social welfare. Thus, L. T. Hobhouse (1864-1929) the first holder of a chair in sociology at the London School of Economics, was concerned to reconcile Liberalism and the philosophy of evolution with the demands of social welfare. In this he attacked Bernard Bosanquet, a philosopher and prominent figure in the C.O.S., in his book *The Metaphysical Theory of the State* (1908). Hobhouse had the liberal optimistic view that progress resulted from the interplay of the actions and reactions of individuals and groups, and that evolution meant an increasing command over nature by means of more conscious and deliberate action. Thus men, through the state, could take action to increase social welfare, for harmony in a society was based upon co-operation rather than upon the exploitation and competition which many forms of Social Darwinism implied.

## Social reform and American social work

Although social workers in Britain at the turn of the century were forced to look at environmental factors more closely than original C.O.S. conceptions of 'deserving' and 'undeserving' clients implied, they failed, partly because of the dominance of the C.O.S. establishment, to develop knowledge of their own about social conditions in a systematic way, or to borrow much from the developing fields of sociology. This contrasts markedly with the development of American social work at the time, culminating in

7

the strong sociological orientation of Mary Richmond's *Social Diagnosis* published in 1917.

Although sociology was first used in the United States to defend slavery in the South, after the Civil War it concerned itself increasingly with the consequences of industrialisation, with alcholism, immigration, crime, poverty and a multitude of economic questions. Sociology became intimately connected with social reform and in 1865 the American Social Science Association was formed, with interests in both sociological facts and social amelioration. The interest in social reform led to the formation of the National Prison Association in 1870 and to the National Conference of Charities and Corrections in 1874, which became the National Conference of Social Work in 1918. In 1906 the American Sociological Society was formed marking the beginning of the differentiation between academic interest in the social sciences on the one hand, and social work and social reform on the other.

Social workers in the American charity organisation movement were originally as influenced by individualistic explanations of poverty as were their British counterparts. Nevertheless, the face to face contact with clients which had been emphasised by Octavia Hill's principle of using personal influence and friendship in tackling poverty, tended in the end to make American social workers look increasingly at environmental influences on poverty. Unfettered by the rigidity of the London C.O.S. American social workers were therefore able to take a real interest in the explanations of social problems which early Ameriman sociologists were currently putting forward. Thus, Charles Ellwood (1873-1946) maintained that sociology had meaning only if it contributed to the cause of social reform and a contemporary, E. A. Ross, attacked a variety of social evils in his book *Sin and Society* (1907). Of particular interest to the social worker of this time was the

8

work of C. H. Cooley (1864-1929). Cooley saw life as a whole whose parts were linked together and supplemented each other. He emphasised the fact that man develops his own personality only within society and that his ego was a 'looking glass' ego reflecting its appearance in the minds of others. Without society, Cooley maintained the ego could not develop.

## *Mary Richmond's* Social Diagnosis

American sociology was beginning to provide a conceptual framework for looking at man in society and it is within this context that Mary Richmond's contribution to social work theory may be seen. Mary Richmond's sociological orientation may have been due in part to her lack of knowledge of the more recent developments in psychological theory in the United States, resulting in her inability to provide any real guide to treatment and the inadequacy of her attempt via 'characterology' to link personality to environment. *Social Diagnosis* contained not one reference to the work of Freud.

Mary Richmond laid great stress on the importance of social factors in the social worker's understanding of the individual and at the beginning of her book quotes approvingly from J. J. Putnam :

> One of the most striking facts with regard to the conscious life of any human being is that it is interwoven with the lives of others. It is in each man's social relations that his mental history is written, and it is in his social relations likewise that the causes of the disorders that threaten his happiness and his effectiveness and the means of securing his recovery are to be mainly sought. (Richmond, 1917)

Mary Richmond emphasised the importance of collecting

and studying social facts in her scheme of problem solving in social work. She saw social evidence as consisting of 'any and all facts as to personal or family history which, taken together, indicate the nature of a given client's social difficulties'. The importance of the client's family and his total social environment was constantly stressed, for 'as society is now organised, we can neither doctor people nor educate them, launch them into industry nor rescue them from long dependence, and do these things in a truly social way without taking their families into account'. Robinson (1939), discussing Mary Richmond's work from the vantage point of the late 1930's saw particular significance in this 'sociological phase' of casework which preceded the 'psychological phase' of the 1920's and 1930's. In Mary Richmond's work the problem of maladjustment was located in the environment, an externalisation of problems which Robinson saw as the 'worker's projection of her own problems and her own need to solve it on her material'. On the other hand, the 'psychological phase' beginning in the 1920's enables the social worker to see the problem of maladjustment in more subjective terms and the cause of problems is sought in the meaning of the individual's own experience and in the individual himself. With the 'psychological phase' the social worker becomes 'lost in identification with the problems of other human beings'. From the standpoint of the 1960's this may still look to us as fair comment on the characteristic drawbacks of both the 'sociological' and the 'psychological' phases in social work.

## The divergence of sociology and social work

Already, when Mary Richmond's *Social Diagnosis* was being published the paths of sociology and social work were diverging. There appear to have been several reasons for this. In the first place, American sociology with its emphasis upon the role of social psychology in the study of social institutions became interested in family, community and cultural studies and in the development of theory. These areas were of great relevance to social work but were largely unrecognised as such by the social workers of the time who were coming under the impact of psychoanalysis. Psychoanalysis was part of the *Zeitgeist* and provided social work with the much needed psychological base which was lacking in Mary Richmond's work. It coincided with the increasingly strong leaning in sociology towards 'pure science' and the conscious effort of many sociologists to avoid the reformist and practical connotations of the earlier period of American sociology. There were exceptions to this concern with 'pure science', for example in criminological and city studies, but the effect of these various trends was largely to divorce social work from sociology for the next twenty to thirty years.

In spite of this divorce the American sociological work of the 1920's and 1930's in both its area of study and its methodology deserved attention from social workers. The publication in 1918 of Park and Burgess' *An Introduction to the Science of Sociology* marked the increased emphasis on sociology as an empirical science with all that this implied in terms of research. This viewpoint was particularly relevant to the kinds of knowledge which social workers need and was demonstrated in the classic study by Znaniecki and Thomas *The Polish Peasant in Europe and America* (1918-21) the first large scale attempt to apply sociological concepts to contemporary problems of cultural change and social disorganisation in an industrial society.

*The case study approach*

W. I. Thomas, co-author of *The Polish Peasant*, held the

view that social phenomena cannot be interpreted by statistics alone and that in order to understand both behaviour and social values sociology must draw upon what he termed 'behaviour documents'. General social processes should be studied on the basis of individual cases and the 'behaviour documents' required would include biographies, letters, diaries, medical and welfare reports, and newspaper reports. These documents would show how situations are dealt with, where attempts at adaptation have been successful or failed and where changes in behaviour and attitude take place. This sociological understanding of the individual in terms of past adaptation and changes in behaviour has clear parallels with what has been considered the requirements of casework understanding of an individual client. The case study method was widely adopted in American sociology and gave it a reality which can be seen in Thomas' *The Unadjusted Girl* (1923) which attempted to discover why there was a rapid increase in prostitutes in the First World War. Thomas showed that the disorganisation of individual life ran parallel with social disorganisation and that conventional ideas of morality were inadequate to bring about social adjustment because these ideas themselves had become confused.

The anthropological influence on the case study approach in sociology is evident and by the 1920's anthropologists were realising the need to make more explicit their own personal and cultural backgrounds when investigating a culture or sub-culture not their own, a need which has only recently begun to make itself clearly felt among social workers. Anthropologists and sociologists realised that if human behaviour is largely *learned* behaviour, then the investigator cannot assume that he is an impersonal objective reporter of human behaviour. 'If subjectivity is unavoidable it can be made explicit' (Rhys Williams, 1959). The case study approach of the 1930's was used largely to investigate social problems of particular interest to social workers. There was, for example, Ruth Cavan's *Suicide* (1928), the work of Clifford Shaw on delinquency producing books such as *Jack Roller, a Delinquent Boy's Own Story* (1930), *The Natural History of a Delinquent Career* (1931) and *Brothers in Crime* (1936).

## Social ecology

One of the most influential developments in sociology in the 1920's and 1930's was the establishment of 'social ecology', the study of the dependence of the individual and the group on geographical environment, which affects group structure and individual behaviour. Robert Park was the leader of this branch of sociology to which he came from journalism, but before his establishment of the 'Chicago School' a good deal of investigation of American city life and its problems was carried out by social reformers in the early years of the century, following the example of Booth's study of London. These were usually practical studies intended to guide social workers and welfare organisations, such as settlements, in undertaking their work, and the Russell Sage Foundation in New York, which placed Mary Richmond in charge of its Charity Organisation Department, also undertook the task of extending social surveys of cities and perfecting social survey methods.

Under Robert Park's leadership the Chicago School's urban sociological surveys were prolific and had definite reformist implications. The intensive study of Chicago made an important contribution to town planning. Social ecology showed that individuals and their social institutions exist in a definite geographical environment, which, though largely the result of social factors, appears to the inhabitants as entirely natural and has an all pervading influence on their behaviour and attitudes. The idea of the geographical location of sub-cultures in the large cities has subsequently been taken very seriously by social workers and has had important influences on the study of delinquency and community and family life in Britain. The Chicago studies showed that the city both assimilated its inhabitants and segregated them into definite groups which had geographical locations. In the 1920's this assimilation and segregation process was demonstrated in a number of works, such as Roderick Mackenzie's *The Neighbourhood* (1923), F. M. Thrasher's classic study *The Gang* (1927), Louis Wirth's *The Ghetto* (1928) and Clifford Shaw's *Delinquency Areas* (1929).

In the same period Robert and Helen Lynd published one of the best known of urban studies *Middletown* (1929). This was an attempt to give an account of a small Middle West town by means of observing it on the spot with interviews, questionnaires, and other anthropological techniques. The second of the Lynd's studies *Middletown in Transition* (1937) was of the same town but concentrated upon one family to show the effect which the Great Depression had on the social structure of Middletown and on the outlook and behaviour of its inhabitants. However, anthropological influence did not only show itself in the work of the Lynds but had a more widespread influence on American sociology of the 1920's and 1930's. In particular, the influence of cultural anthropology showed itself in a characteristic approach to the analysis of social systems, an approach which attempted to analyse a society in terms of its function. This *functionalist* approach, which was later to dominate American sociology, selected for study the basic requirements which had to be satisfied if a social system (whether group or society) was to continue to exist. With this approach functions were seen as established patterns of behaviour, and as these functions were essential to the maintenance of the social order, this form of analysis tended to have *status quo* implications in contrast with sociological analyses which emphasised the importance of conflict as a dynamic of social change.

## Robert MacIver's approach

Despite the general divergence of sociology and social work in America in the inter-war years, some points of contact were maintained. In 1931, the sociologist Robert MacIver delivered the Forbes Lectures to the New York School of Social Work, published in the same year under the title *The Contribution of Sociology to Social Work*. As one of the very few attempts by a sociologist to examine the relationship between the two disciplines it deserves attention here. MacIver emphasised that sociology had no direct therapeutic implications for social work, but that it provided 'the basis for the development of that social philosophy which must integrate the thinking of the social worker, which must control the direction and illuminate the goal of his activity'. He makes clear the distinction between sociology as a *science* concerned with social relationships and social work as an *art* whose object is to relieve or remove particular maladjustments from which individuals suffer in specific social situations. Committed as he was to maintaining the scientific status of sociology he emphasised that sociology could not, as a science, prescribe practice or reform, but only suggest how social problems develop and how, if change is desired, this might be undertaken. It was up to the social worker to make *decisions* about coping with social problems, for social work 'enters boldly into the sphere of values'. 'Science is not a ready reckoner,' he wrote, 'it never offers immediate solutions to the problems of living.'

In considering the contribution of sociology to the amelioration of social problems, MacIver, writing at the

time of the Great Depression, was able to provide a sociologist's answer to some of the socio-political doctrines of
the day. He attacked Social Darwinism by showing that
contemporary sociology saw men as essentially bound up
with one another and dependent upon mutual co-operation. He also opposed the 'hereditarian' view, common at
the time, that social problems arose from 'defective stock'
and that therefore environmental improvement and social
work were useless. Sociology, in contrast, shows the complex interaction of social and biological factors and in
particular that environment affects beliefs, motivation and
attitudes. MacIver also attacks both 'extreme individualism' which 'attributes everything to unequal merits and
demerits and nothing to unequal handicaps', and 'left-wing
socialism' which sees the root of all evil in the economic
system and which saw social work as 'a mere makeshift,
a sentimental support for exploitive capitalism'. In answer
to the socialist critique of social work MacIver admits that
most of the problems which the social worker meets are
generated by the economic system, a fact hard to deny at
that time, but maintains that however much the social and
economic system might be improved or revolutionalised,
the personal element in the causation of social problems
would remain.

## Social work and social evolution

Whilst rejecting what he considered to be false socio-
political doctrines, MacIver commended to social workers
a form of social evolutionism which in its liberal intent
had much in common with Hobhouse. Developing the
*Gemeinschaft-Gesellschaft* conceptual framework of Tönnies (see Chapter Two) he writes, 'One important task of
sociology is to discover and trace the trends of social movements. Some at least of these movements reveal an

16

evolutionary character. In other words, they are inevitably bound up with the transition from a more simple to a more complex society.' Social work, then, was largely the consequence of social evolution, springing from the modern detachment of the individual and the small family group from the sustaining services of the neighbourhood and local community. Social work was part of the new complex industrial society and its function that of mitigating the effects of the breakdown of intimate community support and the values which sustained this support, at the same time assisting social change and the adaptation to new social conditions. MacIver argued for what was to become the 'New Deal' philosophy that the state must be responsible for establishing minimum conditions of life for its citizens. Public service must increasingly replace voluntary effort especially in the relief of poverty, and social work must become more specialised to cope with the increased specialisation of social institutions and the greater complexity of society in general.

When the 'New Deal' philosophy was in fact implemented in the United States, one of its side effects was apparently to decrease the interest of many American social workers in the environmental factors which caused social problems. Prior to the 'New Deal', voluntary social work agencies were used by the U.S. government to distribute financial aid but after 1935 public agencies took over financial relief giving, thus freeing the voluntary social work agencies to 'develop their technical interest in the psychology of the individual' (Wilensky and Lebeaux, 1958). It was largely to the voluntary family casework agencies that professionally-trained social workers were recruited and it was in this particular kind of setting that American casework theory, with its emphasis on individual psychopathology, thrived. The voluntary agencies often tended to neglect the hard social realities which faced the under-staffed and under-trained public agencies.

## The influence of psychoanalysis

While social work of the 1930's was being heavily influenced by psychoanalysis, so also was sociology itself through developments in the field of cultural anthropology. Margaret Mead in *Sex and Temperament in Three Primitive Societies* (1935) introduced Freudian concepts into her work and various analyses were made of personality differences in different societies by reference to child-rearing practices. Abram Kardiner in *The Psychological Frontiers of Society* (1945) used psychoanalytic concepts to suggest that child-rearing practices and family organisation institutionalised in a particular society functioned to produce a basic personality type characteristic of that society. The Neo-Freudians, such as Karen Horney and Erich Fromm also did much to influence sociology in the 1940's and 1950's. Erich Fromm's *The Fear of Freedom* (1942) with its combination of psychoanalytic and Marxist theory was a study of the authoritarian personality, a study which led to extensive research into the location of authoritarian personalities in the social structure, that is in the major institutions and groups in society. (Adorno, 1950).

## Theory and empiricism

What has been described so far of American sociological work was largely empirical in its nature and as such particularly attractive to social workers who feel that they can add to their theoretical framework of psychoanalytic concepts material from sociological work of a descriptive kind. In sociology generally in the last twenty years, however, there has beeen increasing concern over the dangers of narrow empiricism and of the neglect of theory about

18

society as a whole. This concern is of importance to social workers for they also need theoretical concepts if they are to use sociological knowledge effectively in their work. Reliance on descriptive material on family organisation, for example, will not of itself bring about an integration of sociological and psychological concepts necessary for a thorough social diagnosis of family problems. Social workers will have to be as familiar with sociological analysis as they are at present with psychoanalysis if unified theories of causation are to be developed.

Reinhard Bendix has been one sociologist who has been concerned with the relative lack of theoretical work in American sociology. In his *Social Science and the Distrust of Reason* (1951) he sees sinister implications in the emphasis on fact finding, since this tends to make sociology uncritical of the existing structure of society, whereas sociological theory allows for its relatively detached examination. This argument has parallels with the suggestion that under the influence of psychoanalysis social work has been so concerned with the development of technical skill that it has failed to meet its professional obligation to provide a critique of the social structure which generates social problems. C. Wright Mills, a fierce critic of the American sociological establishment, condemns in *The Sociological Imagination* (1959) both the 'abstracted empiricism' which Bendix complains of and also the 'grand theory' of sociologists such as Talcott Parsons. Mills sees much of the theoretical work of American sociologists as ideologically committed to the *status quo*, especially that which rests upon a functionalist approach to sociological analysis.

*Parsons and Merton*

Talcott Parsons has been a most influential figure in the

development of sociological theory in America and his work has attracted much attention in Britain also. It is largely through Parsons that interest in the work of the great continental sociologists, especially Max Weber, has been re-awakened, and of particular interest to social workers has been his use of psychoanalytic concepts in theories concerning the socialisation of the child within the family, developed in detail in *Family, Socialisation and Interaction Process* (1955). In his major works *The Structure of Social Action* (1937), *Essays in Sociological Theory* (1949), *The Social System* (1951) and *Economy and Society* (1956) Parsons has developed his analysis of social systems. He sees a social system as a system of relationships between individuals and groups and describes this system in terms of norms of behaviour. His analysis involves a study of roles and the expectation of roles between individuals in a given situation, and his work together with that of Robert Merton has had significant influence on social work theory both in the United States (Olds, 1963) and to a lesser degree in Britain (Howarth *et al.*, 1962).

Parsons' work is of such Teutonic proportions and complexity that some critics have thrown doubt on its value. Thus Mills writes:

> Is grand theory, as represented in *The Social System*, merely verbiage or is it also profound? My answer to this question is: it is only about fifty per cent verbiage: forty per cent is well-known textbook sociology. The other ten per cent, as Parsons might say, I am willing to leave open to your own empirical investigations. My own investigations suggest that the remaining ten per cent is of possible—though rather vague—ideological use. (Mills, 1959)

Mills attacks Parsons from his own committed point of view and so his criticism has to be treated with caution.

In view of the use that is made of the theories of Parsons and Merton today it is vital that social workers should be familiar with their major concepts so far as they are relevant to social work practice. A substantial part of the next chapter will be devoted to an exposition of these concepts.

Before concluding this brief survey of American sociology, mention should be made of Robert Merton's particular contribution to the problem of the relationship between facts and theories. In *Social Theory and Social Structure* (1951) he calls for the development of 'middle-range theories' rather than the all-inclusive theoretical systems of sociologists such as Parsons. He wants theories which lie between working hypotheses and all-embracing sociological theories and suggests that it is unrealistic to expect that there can be developed a complete theoretical system into which all the facts from research fall into place. Like the learning theorists in their criticism of psychoanalysis, he attacks theories that attempt to explain all phenomena and prefers theories of limited scope.

In looking historically at the relationship between sociology and social work most attention has been paid to developments in the United States. This has been inevitable because social work theory and professional social work education has been more developed in the United States and because sociology also has thrived more vigorously there.

## Social work and sociology in Britain

Between the World Wars professional social work in Britain developed only very slowly and then primarily in the fields of psychiatric social work and medical social work. Psychiatric social work, beginning in the early 1930's naturally became influenced predominantly by psychology and psychoanalysis rather than by sociology. Timms (1964) has shown that the development of sociological knowledge in psychiatric social work has been very slow and the same could be said of other branches of social work. Goldberg (1955) suggested that emphasis on psychoanalysis had 'led to a temporary neglect of an important former source of knowledge, the social sciences', and remarked that there were very few social scientists in Britain who were interested in motivation and its relationship to group phenomena and that therefore much of the work of British sociologists lacked significance for the social worker.

This is an interesting observation in view of the reputation which British sociology has in following the tradition of Booth and Rowntree in pursuing practical objectives. Its practical objectives have, in fact, been concerned with widespread social amelioration rather than with material more immediately helpful to the practising social worker. Characteristic of British sociological interests were Llewelyn Smith's *New Survey of London Life and Labour* (1930-42) carrying on the Booth tradition, Rowntree's third study of York, *Poverty and Progress* (1942) and Caradog Jones' *Social Survey of Merseyside* (1950). These studies had important implications for social policy, and work such as Mark Abrahams' *Social Surveys and Social Action* (1951) and Ruth Glass' *Social Background of a Plan* (1954) were important in urban development and town planning.

Some recent sociological studies in Britain have had considerable vogue in social work education, especially those which have had definite reformist implication and are practical and descriptive in nature rather than analytical. Foremost among these have been the publications of the Institute of Community Studies, most notably Michael Young and Peter Willmott's *Family and Kinship in East London* (1957) and Peter Townsend's *The Family Life of*

*Old People* (1958). Delinquency studies by some sociologists have had equally important reformist implications such as John Mays' *Growing Up in the City* (1954) and Harriet Wilson's *Delinquency and Child Neglect* (1962). Other studies have laid more emphasis upon the development of theoretical concepts and have also been of importance to social work, including B. M. Spinley's *The Deprived and the Privileged* (1953), Elizabeth Bott's *Family and Social Network* (1957) and Madeline Kerr's *The People of Ship Street* (1958).

In British sociology today the debate over the relative importance of empiricism and theory is proceeding as in the United States. Thus we find Simey (1956) demanding more action research which should be problem centred and concerned with practical results, and Marshall (1963) warning that sociology may be prostituted if sociologists in their eagerness to obtain immediately practical results overlook the real objective of sociology, the development of theory. In the chapters which follow we shall be concerned with both the exposition of theory and the description of empirical material, the twin contributions which sociology can make to the practice of social work.

# 2

# Sociological theory and its applications

We suggested at the beginning of this book that as sociology is the study of social interaction within and between groups, then sociological analysis of the functioning and malfunctioning of groups and their relationships will be of value to the social worker in looking at social problems. In this chapter we will examine sociological approaches to three areas of analysis: society as a whole, social interaction within groups, and the social determinants of personality.

*Sociological approaches to society*

All sociologists have some general picture of how society works, a model which lies in the background of their theories and researches. We have seen already that under the influence of Comte and Spencer early sociologists had an evolutionary model of society within which they viewed social change and social problems. The evolutionary view of society suggested the inherent and inevitable unfolding of stages of development by which society progressed according to some 'natural law'. For Spencer the 'natural law' was derived from Darwin's theories of the survival of the fittest whilst for Marx the 'natural law' concerned the modes of economic production, each stage in society giving way, through revolution, to the next 'higher' stage. Ferdinand Tönnies (1855-1936) in *Gemeinschaft und Gesellschaft* (1887) suggested that more complex rational industrial societies developed from more natural rural communities based upon kinship and neighbourliness, a view which was developed, as we have seen, by Robert MacIver in his approach to the function of social work in industrial society.

Evolutionary theories of society are not held in much esteem in sociology today for there is little evidence to show that modern societies are evolving 'superior' forms of social organisation, or that societies pass through definite predetermined stages of development. Evolutionary models of society may provide some useful hypotheses with which to study the processes of social change, as the Marxist model has, but generally these models have been abandoned in favour of others which provide a more fruitful basis for sociological analysis.

## The structural-functional approach

We saw that the attempt to analyse society in terms of its functions had its roots in cultural anthropology. The structural-functional school of sociology under the leadership of Talcott Parsons (1951), is concerned with the way in which social life in any society is maintained and carried forward in spite of the complete turnover of the membership of society which occurs in every generation. The emphasis of this approach is not upon change, but upon the way in which the social system is maintained and continued. Society continues because it has the *structure*, by which the *functions* or needs of society are met. One of the institutions which make up the structure of society is the family which by socialising the child into the culture of society (its ideas, values, knowledge and attitudes) helps to maintain the cultural patterns which bind society together. In this view, the family is seen as a means by which society is maintained, for it provides a secure system of relationships for the purpose of sexual reproduction and child rearing. It is through the family that cultural values are transmitted, that the individual's superego is formed (to use psychoanalytic terminology) and the family is therefore characteristically concerned with the maintenance of tradition and the continuance of the *status quo*. Where social change is very rapid and cultural values are uncertain the family's task of socialisation becomes a difficult one.

As part of the structural-functional approach, with its emphasis on maintenance and continuity, there has developed an equilibrium model of society derived from the concept of homeostasis in human physiology which sees the body as a self-adjusting mechanism. Society, on this model, makes more or less automatic adjustments in the face of conflict or social disorganisation in order to bring itself back into equilibrium. Thus, society is seen as essentially stable with conflict as an aberration which, once resolved, allows society to regain its previous stability. Human behaviour is derived from the common values underlying society, transmitted by the socialisation process and orientated towards its functioning. The conditioning and limitation of the individual's actions, which the social control exercised by society and its members entails, is directed towards his own interests, which are bound up with the maintenance and continuation of society.

An illustration can be given of the way in which the self-adjusting equilibrium model of society can be used to look at the development of the social services and social work. In recent years in Britain considerable attention has been given to the social problems of child neglect and delinquency which appear to surround the 'problem family'. Such families and the problems which they give rise to produce a stress on society which suggests a disequilibrium in the social system. 'Problem families' are not performing the task of socialising their children in accordance with the values of society and various institutions such as property are threatened by the delinquency which results from the development of values at variance with the predominant values of society. Society takes various steps to eliminate this source of strain. It strengthens the mechanisms of social control by developing family casework services whose essential purpose is to improve the parents' ability and desire to socialise their children in accordance with the predominant values. It strengthens the social control exercised by other agencies also, by improving juvenile court organisation, and increasing the residential facilities for delinquents. In these and other ways society regulates the problems arising from deviance and so attempts to restore equilibrium in the social system.

Clearly, this is a particularly static way of viewing society and open especially to the objection that it fails to take into account the positive function of conflict as a vehicle of social change. However, the structural-functional approach with its emphasis upon the importance of shared values as a condition of social stability draws attention to the significance of social disorganisation and the breakdown of social relationships in the etiology of social problems such as delinquency and mental illness. Social Disorganisation Theory (Rose, 1957) sees social problems as occurring when individuals and groups interact in the absence of common values. Absence of common values may be due either to individuals and groups coming into contact for the first time or because under certain conditions there is a weakening of social bonds. This approach assumes that socialisation is a matter of degree and that inadequate socialisation may lead to a weakening of the norms which bind men together in social relationships. Durkheim (1897) in his classic study of suicide, shows that one form of suicide is due to a weakening of social norms brought about by rapid social changes in complex industrial societies. 'Whenever serious readjustments take place in the social order, whether or not due to a sudden growth or an unexpected catastrophe, men are more inclined to self-destruction.' Faris and Dunham (1939) in an ecological study of mental disorder suggested that social isolation was a major cause of schizophrenia. Kobrin (1951) produces evidence that urban areas with high delinquency rates are characterised not by the dominance of either conventional or criminal values but rather by a conflict of norms and values.

*The conflict theory approach*

We have suggested that the drawback of the structural-functional approach to society is that it provides only a static model and neglects the dynamics of social change. Also, it is open to the criticism that it fails to recognise the unequal distribution of power in society, for what might be functional for one group in society may not be for another. The conflict school of sociology, with precursors such as Marx and present exponents Dahrendorf (1959) and Coser (1956), sees society essentially in terms of conflict between diverse and sometimes opposing interests. Conflict is seen as normal and the progenitor of social change as well as the cause of social problems. With this model of society, social control is seen as likely to be functional for only the dominant groups in society and a consensus of values is explicitly ruled out. Values are sometimes seen as the superstructure reflecting the socio-economic substructure in which the individual occupies a particular social position. Social problems are produced because the goals which men strive for are not equally available for all, and as some inevitably fail to achieve the goals, conflict is due to competition for scarce resources. Dahrendorf (1959) maintains that for any dynamic theory of social change no other starting-point than Marx is possible. He criticises the structural-functional school on the grounds that it accounts for change within a social system primarily in terms of its adaption to the conditions of the environment and fails to recognise that social systems have disruptive as well as integrative elements within them. We need, Dahrendorf suggests, both an 'integrative' theory on structural-functional lines which accounts for stability and consensus of values, and a 'power' or conflict theory which recognises that societies are sometimes explosive mixtures held together by force.

We may illustrate the conflict theory approach to social problems by turning again to a consideration of the position of the 'problem family' in Britain today. Marx, with his theory of class conflict, saw the working class as being *in* society but not *of* it, as alienated from society as a whole. He predicted that the class structure would be simplified and that class conflict would manifest itself in a total confrontation of bourgeoisie and proletariat. Marx's picture fitted the facts of the nineteenth and early twentieth century capitalism, but the class struggle in Britain has been diluted since then by the institutionalisation of conflict via the trade union and political parties. by increased prosperity, and by the development of social rights with the 'Welfare State'. The British working class today is no longer so alienated from society, and its values and patterns of consumption may be nearer those of the middle class, although Lockwood (1963) and Goldthorpe (1965) have shown that the working-class trend to middle-class cultural patterns is less marked than is sometimes sug-

29

gested. The advent of television and the development of other forms of mass media have, however, certainly resulted in less cultural isolation for the working class. Some of these social and economic changes have not applied equally to all sections of the working class. The lowest socio-economic stratum of the working class has not benefitted relatively by the generally increased material prosperity of society. Much unskilled work is insecure and in some occupations wages have remained at or below subsistence level. This stratum of society has not been able to take advantage of improved educational facilities which place a premium on qualities that are culturally alien to it.

Here, we might say, is a stratum of society alienated from society as a whole, competing unsuccessfully for scarce resources and producing a disproportionate number of social problems especially those of poverty, illness, child neglect and delinquency (Leonard, 1964). This stratum of socially and economically disadvantaged individuals and families does not form a group conscious of its common manifest interests whose goal is to attack the existing power structure. Rather, it forms a quasi-group of people who have similar latent interests in changing the *status quo*, but with no class consciousness to make this interest manifest. The dominant groups in society are concerned to dilute the conflict without making any substantial change in the socio-economic structure, and so individuals within this stratum who come into conflict with the wider society are termed 'maladjusted', 'deviant' or 'abnormal' and therefore the object of social work. Within this analysis social work is seen as a means by which society can ensure that underprivileged individuals are manipulated into adjusting to their position in society.

It will be evident that conflict theory provides potentially a more radical analysis of social problems than does the structural-functional approach. The radicalism of this approach may, however, be used ideologically for the Right as well as for the Left. Thus in the field of criminology, Vold (1958) has argued in a way strongly reminiscent of Hobbes, that crime is 'minority behaviour', a form of conflict inherent in society in which laws represent the will of the stronger. Criminals are those 'without sufficient public support to dominate and control the police power of the state. Criminals often become involved in the serious business of politics and control of the police power of the state for their own protection. This is "pressure politics" in the interests of organised crime.' Vold makes clear the ideological implications of this approach when he points out that murder and violations against property are a commonplace accompaniment of political rebellion. Most crime should therefore be seen as *political behaviour*, an attack on the fabric of society and resisted as such.

Both structural-functional theory and conflict theory have something to offer the social worker who attempts to look at the significance of his work in the context of society's approach to social problems. Conflict theory with its emphasis upon economic factors and the distribution of power acts as a valuable counter-balance to the tendency in social work to take society and its fundamental socio-economic institutions for granted. On the other hand, the structural-functional approach, especially in developing role theory, is beginning to have an important influence on social work theory. In moving the focus of attention from society as a whole to the analysis of social interaction within groups, we shall be drawing primarily upon the structural-functional approach.

## Social interaction in groups

We may begin the analysis of group interaction by seeing groups, of whatever size from that of society to that of the two-man group of the casework relationship, as social systems which involve some degree of co-operation among its members for the attainment of common goals. This co-operation does not, of course, preclude antagonism and conflict, for in any group there may be co-operation in some areas and conflict in others. The members of a group have rights and obligations which are not carried by those outside the group, and these rights and duties are the rules of behaviour of the group, a pattern of *norms* which govern the behaviour and expectations of the group members. A group consists, essentially, of individuals in their capacity as members; because he is a member of several groups (family, trade union, etc.) the individual does not relate to other group members as a whole person but only in his capacity as a member of a particular group. This emphasis on viewing individuals as *group members* is important in social work for it draws attention to the kinds of behaviour which are appropriate in different kinds of groups. 'Appropriate behaviour' in any group is defined by the norms of the group. These are said to be institutionalised when they are widely accepted in a group and deeply inculcated into the personalities of its members. Obviously, there are degrees of institutionalisation, and social workers are particularly interested in those circumstances where there is a lack of conformity to group norms which leads to behaviour which is deviant so far as the group is concerned.

All members of a group are not expected to behave in the same way, for the group norms apply to members according to their *social position* in the group and determine the behaviour appropriate to each social position. As an example, we may take the position of a caseworker in a social work agency. The caseworker is expected to have and use certain knowledge and skills, such as the ability to assess social problems and knowledge of the appropriate social services. There are two kinds of norms involved here. In the first place, there are the *technical and professional norms* governing the correct use of casework knowledge and skill. In the second place there are the *social norms* governing the social work agency's expectation that the caseworker, in performing his job, will conform to the technical and professional norms. If the caseworker deviates from the professional norms by becoming emotionally over-involved with a client, his supervisor may draw attention to this by reference to those norms. The caseworker, on the other hand, because of his social position in the group, has a right to expect the performance of certain tasks by others in the social work agency. He may expect clerical assistance from the secretarial staff and time given for consultation over difficult cases by a senior caseworker in the agency. These rights are equally norms applied by the caseworker to other members of the agency, for what are one member's rights are another member's obligations and the smooth functioning of the agency requires that each member of it should know and accept a considerable part of the whole normative pattern of the group.

From this example we can see that a social position has two parts, namely, *status*, which are the rights which an individual has within the group, and *role*, which are the obligations which an individual has within the group. The concept of role has been used in many different ways (see Neiman and Hughes, 1961) and is often used to denote the whole social position, for every role has a status and every status a role. The member of a group occupying a particular social position usually interacts with several other people occupying many different social positions. In order to analyse the interrelatedness of social positions Merton (1957) has developed the concept of *role-set*.

The term role-set refers, firstly, to the complex of other

social positions with which any particular social position is characteristically connected. Secondly, it is used when a particular occupant of a social position is taken as the point of reference, in which case his role-set is the total number of occupants of the social positions with whom he must normally interact. As an example of the *role-set* concept we may take, once again, the position of the caseworker in the social work agency. The caseworker employed by a local authority interacts with a number of people as he performs his role, among them fellow social workers, senior local authority staff, social work students in training, local authority committee members, and clients. These positions represent the role-set for the position of a local authority caseworker and for a particular caseworker the actual people occupying these positions constitute his role-set. The caseworker's role in relation to each position in the role-set involves different patterns of behaviour and his social position is not perceived in the same way by the occupants of all the social positions in his role-set. Senior administrative staff in the local authority do not expect to be 'caseworked', that is treated like clients by professional social work staff. Students and clients perceive a particular caseworker differently because of the different role relationship between them.

Returning to a consideration of the norms which govern the role and status of the member of any group we may ask under what conditions norms become institutionalised. It would seem that this occurs when a large number of group members accept the norms, when many of those who accept the norms incorporate them into their own value system, and when the norms are *sanctioned*, that is expected to guide member's behaviour. Of course, like institutionalisation, internalisation, the incorporation of norms into the personality, is a matter of degree: some norms are taken more seriously than others. In many social work agencies confidentiality is taken more seriously than up-to-date case recording. Conformity to institutionalised norms is usual in any group both because of the internalised need for the norms experienced by group members and because of the external sanctions which bring about conformity. Sanctions are necessary because however well institutionalised a norm may be there will be group members who are tempted to depart from it. Thus social control is exercised both externally through the direct application of sanctions and internally by the individual foreseeing in his imagination the responses of others to his actions.

Within a group an individual may find himself subject to conflicting norms because he occupies a social position which is perceived differently by different group members, himself included. In *role conflict* two groups or sub-groups are brought into a relationship with each other through the fact that the same person occupies a role in one of the groups which is incompatible with a role he occupies in another. If, for example, we take the family group as consisting of various sub-groups such as husband-wife and mother-child, then we can see that the mother of a sick child who needs special attention may experience role conflict due to the incompatible role expectations of the two sub-group members, husband and child respectively. Nursten (1964) has illustrated the role conflict inherent in being both a grammar school boy and a member of a working-class adolescent group. The result of role conflict is always deviation because it is not possible to meet fully the conflicting norms and role expectations of each group : even compromise involves some deviation. The relationship between the different roles a person carries need not be conflicting but may be reinforcing, that is, one role may reinforce motivation to conform to another role. An example of this is the reinforcement of a man's occupational

35

role when he is a father, because part of the paternal role consists of supporting the family materially.

## Role theory in casework

Having presented some of the elements in the analysis of groups in terms of role relationships we should mention the specific use to which role theory may be put in casework. Perlman (1957), for example, examines the casework implications of the fact that an individual's behaviour is both shaped and judged by the expectations which both he and his culture have invested in the major social positions he occupies with their respective roles and statuses. As the nature of an individual's social interaction is reflected in his role performance, so we may expect that the client of a social work agency will generally be someone who has difficulty in performing one of his vital roles. This difficulty may be due to the fact that he is emotionally unable to meet the demands of one of his roles, such as that of father or husband, because of some personality problem. Alternatively, difficulty in role performance may be due to the fact that the same man is unable to reconcile successfully the role of son which he has had for the whole of his life, with the role of husband which he has only recently acquired. Again, an individual may be unable to perform a role effectively because of the lack of the necessary equipment to carry out the role. Thus a mother may be prevented from carrying out her role because of low income and inadequate housing.

The use of role theory in casework demands that the social worker should both see the client in his total cultural setting in order to assess the demands made upon him by his role set, and attempt to identify those stresses which have their origin in role conflict. Perlman (1960) and Rosenblatt (1963) have both used role theory to explore the problems which arise if caseworker and client have different but unexpressed expectations of each other's role at the beginning of the casework relationship. Social workers are familiar with the problems of deciding the objectives of the initial interview with a client. Very often the social worker views the initial interview as one in which he explores the ground with the client in order to see whether the social work agency can help the person being interviewed. In other words, he sees the role of interviewee not as that of actual client, but of potential client or applicant for the service which the social work agency provides. The interviewee, on the other hand, may see her own role as that of actual client and she therefore expects that her problems will be taken up and worked on immediately. In terms of the analysis of group interaction, common goals have not yet clearly been established and, therefore, the norms which will govern the behaviour and expectations of the two individuals in the group and lead to the establishment and common acceptance of their respective roles, have yet to be formulated. Of course, in the caseworker-client relationship, the caseworker enters into the system of social interaction with fairly clear ideas, within general limits, of the goals, norms and roles appropriate to this particular kind of social system. Her aim will be to induce the client to take the role reciprocal to her own 'helping' role, and to accept within broad limits that the goals of this system of interaction are to be defined in a way which is in line with the aims and functions of the social work agency. The caseworker, for example, will resist the client's attempt to induce him to take the role of over-possessive mother substitute as he will see this role as inappropriate. The caseworker may deal with the client's deviation from the group norms by applying sanctions such as emotional or physical withdrawal, manifest or latent hostility, or a reduction in the number of

37

occasions on which the social interaction takes place.

The use of role theory in examining the caseworker-client relationship highlights the problem which an individual faces in accepting the social position of client. One may expect that for the adult hospital patient, for example, the norms of autonomy and self-sufficiency which govern his behaviour and expectations in the wider social systems of the family and society, will clash with the new hospital norms of enforced dependency. Thus a patient may refuse the help of a medical social worker because the demands of the role of client would require him to acknowledge further that he is no longer able to care for himself. On the other hand, as Parsons and Fox (1960) have pointed out there may be for some individuals considerable attraction in choosing a 'sick role' as a means of escape from the pressures of occupational and family roles. What emerges from all this is a suggestion that the caseworker has a function in discussing and clarifying the respective roles of caseworker and client and the norms governing the behaviour of each. The means by which this is done will, of course, depend upon innumerable factors, including the personality of the client, the nature of his problem and the skill and experience of the caseworker. After discussing the care with which any role clarification with a client must be undertaken, Rosenblatt (1963) writes:

> The procedure of informing the client of the set of norms governing his role, may, however, decrease the dropout rate if this information serves (a) to decrease the strain created in the client by the conflict of roles, or (b) to identify the strains he will have to bear if he assumes the client role, strains that the client usually senses. In short, any discussion of norms with a client should be geared to his current needs and should not be based on a rigid formula.

We should return now once again to our wider consideration of social interaction in groups. The applications of role theory in social work will be examined further in the next chapter when we consider the sociological approach to family interaction.

## The functional problems of groups

Theorists of the structural-functional school have suggested that all systems of social interaction have to deal with certain kinds of functional problems if they are going to continue to exist as independent entities. The first problem is termed *pattern-maintenance* and *tension-management*. The structure of any social group must be maintained by the units of the group learning the normative patterns of the group, internalising them to some degree or in any case treating them with respect. In the family group the maintenance of the normative pattern is achieved by the mechanisms of socialisation by which the cultural patterns become incorporated into the personalities of the family members. The mechanism of socialisation serves both the family itself and the wider society, for if socialisation is inadequate then the individual is less likely to accept the normative pattern of society. Again, if we take professional social work to be an occupational sub-system then we may view social work education as socialisation into a particular professional sub-culture. That this is so is evident from the emphasis that is placed in social work education on the incorporation of appropriate professional values and attitudes, as well as the acquiring of knowledge and the learning of particular skills. Through insistence on certain standards of training professional social work associations attempt to maintain a pattern of norms, though, unlike the legal or medical professions, they have not yet developed effective sanctions with

39

which to exercise social control over those who deviate.

Group members are often subject to emotional disturbance and distraction which has to be managed by the group if it is to continue effectively. In any group an individual or sub-group will have to undertake the management of tension. In the family, the member who manages tension is usually the mother, who in western society, Parsons (1955) has suggested, is expected to take a predominantly 'expressive' role, being caring, loving and understanding in relation to the family members' emotional difficulties. The family as a whole, through the encouragement and care of its members, performs the function of tension management in relation to the total society. In a social work agency, as in many other groups, the role of tension manager may be assumed informally by a particular member of the agency who may occupy almost any position in the organisational hierarchy but who is someone to whom others will go to talk over a problem informally.

The second functional problem for groups is that they must be *adapted* to the environment, be able to meet any exigencies which may occur, in order that they may meet the third problem, the *attainment of common goals*. Every permanent group needs to have some division of labour, some differentiation of roles among the group members, in order that adaptation may proceed relatively smoothly. In the family group, the father may be seen as taking an 'instrumental' role for he is 'supporter' of the family and a major channel of interaction between the family and the outside world. The father is expected to be a 'good provider' and to secure for the family a 'good position' in the community; it is through the father's occupation that the social status of the family is determined. In any group the attainment of goals depends upon the extent to which the group members are able to co-operate together, co-operative effort which demands the solving of the fourth problem, group *integration*.

The members of any group must be loyal to one another and to the group as a whole, and so the group has to maintain solidarity and morale. There must be a willingness among group members to give themselves to specific undertakings and the co-operative activities which require group integration depend upon effective decision making and a hierarchy of authority. Here, as Weber (1947) saw, it is important to distinguish between power and authority, for the latter is essentially legitimised power. In the group context, power is the ability to induce others to accept orders, but the power is legitimised if it is in line with the values held by the other group members. The hierarchy of authority is immediately evident in the formal structure of organisations, such as factories, schools and social work agencies. In less formally structured groups the problem of integration has still to be met and so informal leaders who exercise the necessary authority evolve from the group itself. Within the family, the actual distribution of authority will depend upon the particular culture within which the family exists, but in every culture some family members, the children, will be expected to be subordinate to other family members, the parents. Finally, in the interests of integration there has to be not only social control to deal with violations of group norms, but also some social arrangements for the settling of disputes about norms or about conflicts of interest. In the family, quarrelling siblings may bring their dispute to a parent for arbitration, just as conflicting groups in industry may also seek arbitration.

## The Social determinants of personality

The remainder of this chapter is to be devoted to taking

sociological analysis a step further by beginning to explore the relationship which exists between society and its various sub-groups on the one hand, and the individual on the other. As we have seen, the socialisation process is central to the relationship between the individual and the social group. It is through this process that the young human being acquires the values and knowledge of his group, and learns the social roles appropriate to it. In this way man's biological drives are directed into socially valuable channels. The relationship between the individual and society was seen by Freud in essentially negative terms. Early psychoanalytic theory emphasised the power of the individual's instinctual needs and the harmful effects of their frustration by social restraint. With the later development of ego-psychology more emphasis was placed upon the adaptation of man to society and on the beneficial effects of socialisation.

Sociology, in contrast, tends to emphasise man's rationality rather than his irrationality. Man is seen as essentially rational in that he pursues those personal and cultural goals which his culture and time define as appropriate. From the sociological point of view it is clear that if men could not count on and predict the actions of other men social life would simply disappear. Thus man is committed to mutual adaptation and adjustment to attain both his own goals and the goals of society and other social groups which he has internalised and made his own. From this point of view personality, although it may possess innate qualities, is essentially a function of the structure and value system of numerous social groups up to and including society. One way in which sociologists have attempted to explore the relationship between personality and society is by means of typologies of personality. These are theoretical models which attempt to explain the differences of personality characteristics in different societies by reference to the nature of the societies themselves. We shall examine two such typologies, those of Tönnies and Riesman.

## Tönnies' typology

Ferdinand Tönnies in *Gemeinschaft und Gesellschaft* (1957) developed a typology which had considerable influence. He suggested that the simplest and most general unit of social life is the *social relationship*, implying interdependence and the will of one person influencing that of the other. There are two kinds of social relationship resting on two kinds of human willing: the *rational will*, (*Kürwille*) which denotes social relationships characterised by the individual's motives being centred upon the calculation of means and the appropriateness of means to ends; and the *natural will* (*Wesenwille*), which denotes those social relationships which are characterised by their unconditional nature, such as the relationship between mother and child. These latter relationships may be positive or negative, loving or hating. Society, which consists of the total complex of social relationships, is itself characterised by the type of will predominant in it. Thus Tönnies arrived at a construction of two types of society reflecting two types of personality: the *Gemeinschaft* which reflected the natural will and the *Gesellschaft* reflecting the rational will. A *Gemeinschaft* emerges from natural relationship, as does the kinship group, and its members tend to have a common relation to the soil. The dominant social relationships are characterised by fellowship, kinship and neighbourliness, whilst religion and cultural mores are among the major types of social control. A *Gesellschaft*, on the other hand, comes with the emergence of the state and the development of capitalist, middle-class society in which the original qualities of the *Gemeinschaft* may be lost. The dominant social relationships of the cosmopolitan city life of the *Gesellschaft* centre on exchange and rational calculation, the characteristic form of wealth is money, and social control is effected primarily through legislation and public opinion.

Clearly, there are nostalgic implications in Tönnies work; a romanticised image of rural community life and of the personality type characteristic of it recurs frequently in community studies. Nevertheless, the distinction he draws has a good deal of validity, suggesting in urban planning and social work, especially group and community work, the need to counter the anonymity and alienation of large city life. Thus, there is a movement in our society both to preserve the existing pockets of *Gemeinschaft* life and to develop this type of community by careful urban planning and the encouragement of neighbourhood and community consciousness. Young and Willmott sum up the need to preserve the *Gemeinschaft* of parts of London in the following words:

> The sense of loyalty to each other amongst the inhabitants of a place like Bethnal Green is not due to the buildings. It is due far more to the ties of kinship and friendship which connect the *people* of one household to the people of another. In such a district community spirit does not have to be fostered, it is already there. If the authorities regard this spirit as a social asset worth preserving, they will not uproot more people, but build new houses around the social groups to which they already belong. (Young and Willmott, 1957)

*Riesman's typology*

David Riesman's *The Lonely Crowd* (Riesman, 1958; Riesman and Glazer, 1952) provides a three-fold typology of personality representing different models of conformity

44

or response to social control. Like Tönnies, Riesman begins by considering the type of society where social control is minimal. In this *tradition-directed* society conformity is assured by inculcating the young with automatic obedience to tradition in a role defined from birth; the individual is *tradition-directed* and his behaviour is minutely controlled from without by traditional cultural standards, by kinship ties, religion, ceremonials, etc. The tradition-directed man conforms to external standards and is typical of long-settled unchanging societies with a fairly stable ratio of man-to-land combined with great potential for growth. The Middle Ages in western history is seen as a period high in tradition-direction.

A change in the ratio of births to deaths often brings about far reaching changes in tradition-directed society. As population expands the death rate drops, agriculture improves and yields surpluses, and a new personality type comes forward to take advantage of the new opportunities —the *inner-directed* man. Society is now characterised by rapid social mobility, the accumulation of capital, invention and expansion. The *inner-directed* man conforms to internalised controls and has special attitudes to work and leisure. He is the type whose goals are wealth, fame, goodness and achievement; the type of person whom Weber (1958) saw as epitomising the Calvinistic Capitalist of the eighteenth and nineteenth century. Further changes in society bring, Riesman suggests, further changes in the dominant personality type. Death rates fall still further, population declines or becomes static, agriculture is replaced by industry, and hours of work are short while materials and leisure are abundant. In this 'affluent society' increasingly 'other people are the problem not the material environment'. The dominant personality type is *other-directed*, a type who is both the cause and the consequence of industrial society and the rise of the new middle classes.

45

In the other-directed society, men are preoccupied with consumption rather than production, concerned for the 'human factor' in industry, and parental control weakens. Interpersonal relations loom large, and the individual's contemporaries are his source of direction. The individual is concerned not with what traditions or conscience dictate, but with reference groups of various kinds, a situation graphically documented also by Whyte (1956) and Mills (1951). Finally, the more that inter-personal relationships become the centre of an individual's problems, the greater the need society has to develop therapies of various kinds, including psychiatry and social work.

## Personality and culture patterns

Although sociological typologies of personality point in gross terms to the relationship between personality and society, they do not indicate how, through the socialisation process, cultural values are internalised. Consequently, some account of the internalisation of cultural patterns must be given. Kardiner (1945), in developing his theory of basic personality structure, maintains that characteristic unconscious constellations are produced in individuals by child-rearing practices and other 'primary institutions', such as the prevailing form of family organisation in a given culture. The aspects of the culture in which these 'constellations' find expression are in 'secondary institutions' such as art, folk lore, mythology and religion. The basic personality structure in any society is a set of trends which develop in the characters of all individual personalities who have been reared under the same 'primary institutions'. Kardiner's hypothesis can be shown diagrammatically:

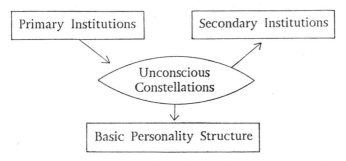

Kardiner tested his hypothesis by an 'exercise in psychopathology' in which he interpreted anthropologists' materials by means of psychoanalytic theory. His studies of simpler societies produced considerable evidence that particular forms of child-rearing institutionalised in the culture produced certain common personality characteristics. The applications of Kardiner's ideas in cross-cultural child-rearing studies will be examined in the next chapter.

Parsons (1963) has given in some detail his views on the way in which the child becomes socialised to his culture using a structural-functional framework, integrated with psychoanalytic concepts. He suggests that internal control over the child's own impulses becomes established through a generalised pattern of sanctions imposed by the mother: the child not only responds to specific 'rewards' but also to the intentions of the mother and so learns to conform to her expectations. In this way the child learns a generalised goal which is not just to gratify his impulses but to please his mother. By identification with the mother the child both learns to act in conformity to a set of norms which are implicit in the mother's behaviour, and to strive for the primary goal—the praise, or love, of the mother. Identification, in Parsons' view, is the process by which the person comes to be inducted into membership of a group through learning to play a role complementary to

47

those of other members in accordance with the normative pattern governing the group. 'The new member,' he writes, 'comes to be *like* the others with respect to their common membership status and to the psychological implications of this—above all the common values there internalised.' For Parsons, then, socialisation into the culture occurs by the child's learning social roles within, initially, the family group and learning his first reciprocal roles through identification with the mother. Identification with the mother also means that the child internalises the mother-child pattern of relationships and so lays the foundation of his capacity to assume a parent's role as well as his own. In this way the child is prepared for adult roles and in particular the parental role he will have to carry if he is eventually to socialise his own child.

# 3

# Personality, family and culture

An important contribution which sociology can make to social work is in the formulation of hypotheses explaining the relationship between the development of personality, the structure and organisation of the family and the nature of the culture within which the individual and the family exist. We have already looked at this relationship within broad theoretical terms which describe the family as a means by which the cultural patterns of a society are transmitted to the individual and thus influence the development of his personality. This relationship needs now to be explored in more detail. As social work becomes more family-centred psychoanalytic concepts alone cannot provide the conceptual framework that is necessary for the development of a thorough understanding of family inter-relationships. As Meyer (1959) has pointed out, traditionally family diagnosis in social work has meant 'keeping in mind' the family whilst the social worker works with one of its members. In recent years social workers have wanted to advance on this and try to understand 'family interaction', as more than the actions of individuals. Family diagnosis is not the result of adding up the assessments of individuals, for the behaviour of one person is simultaneously the cause and effect of the behaviour of

49

another. Bossard and Boll (1960) have summed up the complexity of this interaction as follows: 'With the addition of each person to a family or primary group, the number of persons increases by the simplest arithmetical progression in whole numbers, and the number of interpersonal relationships increase in the order of triangular numbers.' This can be shown diagrammatically:

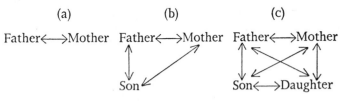

One relationship          Three relationships     Six relationships

We shall begin to penetrate this complexity of relationships by looking at role conflict in the family and the ways in which it may be resolved.

*Role conflict*

Conflict is a normal part of any interaction within groups and, as we have seen, one of the problems which have to be solved by groups is the resolution of such conflict. A framework within which to examine the reasons for conflict and the ways in which it may be resolved has been developed by Spiegel (1960) and will be used to focus our discussion.

The breakdown of roles within a family may occur for several reasons. It may be due to *cognitive discrepancy*, an ignorance of the norms governing the roles, as when adolescent and parent are uncertain of what should be expected of a person who is neither a child nor yet an adult. The birth of the first child in a family may produce

50

uncertainty in both mother and father as to how to perform their new roles, especially when, as is the case today, these roles are themselves undergoing cultural change. A breakdown in roles may also be due to a *discrepancy of goals* when behaviour is directed towards different and potentially conflicting goals by two or more family members. Mother and child frequently have conflicting goals, the child demanding the gratification of its wishes and the mother withholding gratification as part of her task of socialising the child to the demands of the outside world. Again, goal discrepancy may come about through a member being unable to reach the goals which his role requires because of some incapacity such as illness. For example, a husband who is suffering from depression may be impotent and unable to perform his marital role satisfactorily. There may be *allocative discrepancy* when roles are taken in the family which are prohibited by the cultural norms which determine the allocation of roles. For example, the father who adopts the role of seducer of his daughter gives up, at least temporarily, his culturally ascribed role of parent, while the mother may assign to her daughter the role of sexual 'victim' (see Kaufman, Peck and Taguire, 1960). Another reason for the breakdown of roles which we mentioned in the last chapter is called by Spiegel *instrumental discrepancy*, lack of the equipment necessary to carry out the role effectively. The socal worker has considerable difficulty here in deciding, for example, whether a man's unemployment which makes him unable to carry out his role as father effectively, is in fact the result of his rejection of the role of material supporter of the family. Finally, discrepancy may be due to *different cultural values* held by family members which lead to different definitions of their respective roles. This is classically illustrated in second generation cultural conflict between parents and children in immigrant families in which conflicting norms are operating. It is also seen in the incompatible definitions of husband and wife roles which may occur in marriages between people from totally different cultural backgrounds.

How, we may ask, are such conflicts resolved? Spiegel suggests three ways in which this may come about. Firstly, through *role induction* in which the resolution of conflict is achieved by one partner manipulating the other to take a complementary role while making no change in his own role. There are various ways in which such manipulation may take place, but the most universal is that of direct coercion either by the use of physical punishment or by other means. As a manipulative measure a wife may refuse her husband sexual intercourse, or a husband may restrict his wife's housekeeping money. Of course, manipulation may be achieved in more subtle ways by coaxing, by lying and distortion, and by postponing open conflict in the hope that the other will change his mind and fall in with the manipulating partner's wishes. As a method of resolving conflict manipulation is unlikely to be effective in the long run, for there will remain latent conflict due to lack of agreement about the norms governing family behaviour. The social worker is very frequently faced with the demand by a client that he, the social worker, should engage in role induction, helping the client to manipulate other family members without making a change in her own behaviour or expectations. Thus, a father may ask the social worker to help him to make his son behave differently, work harder at school, be less insolent at home, and imply that all would be well if his son changed. Clients, like everyone else, prefer others rather than themselves to change, and sometimes attempt to achieve this by manipulating the social worker. Probation officers are continually seeing wives who want them to use their authority to try to make their husbands change, for conflict is characteristically presented as resulting from the defective role performance of someone else.

Often, social workers meet this demand for manipulation by trying, initially, to induce the client to put himself, in imagination, in the role of the partner in the conflict. The probation officer may say to the complaining wife at some point 'I wonder what your husband felt when this happened?', so beginning the process which Spiegel calls *role reversal*. Role reversal is the first stage towards *role modification* in which resolution is brought about by both partners changing their roles sufficiently to establish complementarity on a new basis. Modification usually takes place after the partners have gained some insight into each other's position, perhaps by laughing at themselves and each other; joking may express in sublimated form the coercive and manipulative techniques just left behind. Subsequently, role modification may be pursued by referring the conflict to a third party, such as another family member, as happens when a sibling conflict is referred to a parent. If the third party is outside the family, such as a social worker, there are various dangers for the family members concerned. A social worker may in effect steer the conflict-resolving process back to manipulation because he becomes identified with one of the partners to the conflict and so prevents a real modification of roles. As we have noted, the partners to a conflict may have referred it to the social worker with the masked intention of gaining support for manipulation whilst protesting their wish to 'see both sides of the problem' and to 'admit their own faults'. If role modification is proceeding satisfactorily, exploration and compromise will be necessary by both partners and it is here that the social worker's role in marital and parent-child conflict is seen *par-excellence*. Any resolution of substantial conflict within a family is likely to involve strains while the family members learn

53

new roles and internalise them, so that social work support may be needed whilst family members adjust to one another.

## The effects of social change

It is worth emphasising at this point the effects of rapid social change on family conflict. Norms governing the distribution of roles within the family have changed so considerably during this century that socialisation in accordance with parental norms may fail to provide the young couple with adequate guidance for the performance of roles in the very different cultural milieu of their adult lives. Many social changes have affected the family in this country, especially those that have taken place in the role and status of women. The more widespread employment of women affects the father's pre-eminent role of breadwinner, whilst a change in the sex ratio of the population is accompanied by a decline in the age of marriage and an increase in the number getting married. People are living longer and so the four generation family may soon become common and have far reaching effects upon family structure. Smaller families, increased longevity, and earlier marriage means that by forty years of age most women have a long period of active life ahead of them without dependent children. Finally, there continues to be considerable changes in the characteristic life styles of the majority of families who are experiencing increased physical and social mobility.

Against this background of social change with its resultant greater ambiguity about sexual and family roles, we can appreciate the problems of role definition and performance which face the young married couple. Marriage represents the final separating out of the sexes and so is bound to be accompanied by anxieties about what is regarded as masculine and what as feminine. Generally, family and marital roles are not as separated as they were in the past and a decline in the support of the extended family demands greater flexibility of role taking and the ability to reverse roles if the family situation demands it. The father, for example, must be more prepared to care for the children when mother is ill or confined. In our society masculine and feminine roles cannot generally be strictly separated whereas in primitive societies and until lately in Western Europe the sexes were rigorously separated except for parts of their lives. Even today in certain communities rigid separation of roles survives and the hardship of the men's lives is considered to justify their very privileged position relative to the women, as the study of the mining community by Dennis, Henriques and Slaughter (1956) shows. However, in general, the whole of the culture of our society is available to both sexes and this may lead to problems of confusion of roles. In particular, the father may be unsure of the norms governing his relationship with his children, for with their apparent demand that he should have a more close intimate relationship less differentiated from that of the mother, these norms may stand in stark contrast with those which governed the relationship between him and *his* father.

## Role distortion

The effect of social change on the father's role in the family may be related to another important source of role conflict, when a person carries two roles which are governed by widely divergent norms. In these cases, the norms governing the predominant role may come to affect the secondary role and distort it. A clear example of this occurs where there is a strong divergence between the norms governing occupational and paternal roles. We have seen that the parents' function in raising their children is to prepare them to become adults capable of assuming the typical adult roles and of being integrated into the social system. Child-rearing is in this way future-orientated, and for fathers it is experience of the occupational world which tells them what attitudes, skills and qualities their sons must have to fit them for the future. For many fathers there is great separation of occupational and home world, a separation which may operate differently for middle-class and working-class fathers.

Aberle and Naegele (1952) in a study of middle-class fathers found that their subjects' occupational role with its emphasis on responsibility, authority, competition and aggressiveness affected their home role which, with its emphasis on emotional warmth, required very different qualities from the same person. These middle-class fathers projected middle-class futures for their sons and thus evaluated their behaviour in terms of traits which would assist or hinder their future life in the competitive occupational world. The values surrounding emotional warmth were played down and fathers evaluated their sons in much the same way as they might colleagues and subordinates at work. Thus, lack of responsibilty, inadequate performance at school, passivity or insufficiently aggressive behaviour, 'childishness', overconformity and excessive tearfulness were all condemned by fathers.

Titmuss (1958) in looking at the effects on the father's role of work in mass production, automated industry, has been concerned with the same problem of role conflict. There are different norms expected of the worker in the factory and the same man at home. In our society 'stability' is heavily stressed as essential to healthy family life and fathers are expected, by social workers and the community in general, to plan for the future success of their children. For the manual worker, however, stability is not stressed and with increased rationalisation and automation comes uncertainty, irregularity and impermanence of work. Loss of status at work can be damaging to a father's role in the family, and where the worker is dominated by the machine there is submission, dependence and loss of initiative. This contrasts in marked fashion with the norms which are expected to govern the man's behaviour as a father, norms which require him to control his affairs rationally, think about his children's future and show his wife tolerance, respect and understanding. The role conflict inherent in this situation may, Titmuss suggests, make the father submissive and lacking in initiative at home, thus continuing his 'factory role', or authoritarian at home, reacting to the domination of the machine by trying to dominate others. The fact that family roles may be distorted by occupation highlights the importance of social workers' knowing more about the work and occupational environment of their clients.

## 'Scapegoating' and the sick role

The roles which have been discussed so far are those which are the necessary consequence of occupying a certain formal position in the family group. In any social group there are also informal roles which are adopted by group members with the explicit or implicit support of the group. Within the family, one such informal role which is of special significance to social workers is that of the scapegoat where one person expresses in his behaviour the conflict which exists in the family. This has been a familiar notion in the field of child guidance, where the disturbed child is frequently seen as a symptom of family pathology. The Canford Families Project, for example (Howarth *et al.*, 1962) was designed to test the hypothesis 'That a child's behaviour at home or at school, which caused con-

E                                                                57

cern to parents or others, would be associated with a problem in the family, particularly in the performance of parental roles'. In the small number of families studied and helped by the Project there was evidence to support this hypothesis, which drew attention to the parent's own disrupted childhood, with its inevitable defective socialisation, and its effect upon their ability to perform parental roles adequately.

If the role of scapegoat is assigned to a child because of the existence of tensions between parents which have not been satisfactorily resolved in other ways, then how is it that a child is chosen and how is he induced to take the role and stay in it? The unconscious purpose of scapegoating, as Vogel and Bell (1960), Bateson (1956), Laing and Esterson (1964), Wynne (1958) and others have shown, is to provide some appropriate object to symbolise the conflict in the family and draw off the tension occasioned by it. The child is an appropriate scapegoat because he is in a relatively powerless position compared with the parents, and is unable to leave the family. Because the child's personality is relatively flexible he can be moulded to adopt the particular role assigned to him by the family, and when he takes on the characteristics which the parents dislike in themselves he becomes symbolically the appropriate object on which the parents may focus their anxieties. Carrying the role of scapegoat tends to interfere with the satisfactory performance of formal roles because of the tensions generated, but it is less disruptive of family life that a child's role performance be disturbed than that a parent's should be. When the child carries out his role as 'problem child', the parents both protest about the behaviour and at the same time often reinforce it. Both parents and child obtain gratification from the symptoms the child develops, for in spite of their protests the parents accept the symptoms and make special arrangements to accommodate them. Thus, the enuretic child may be acting out the repressed wishes of his obsessional mother. Social workers are faced, as Vogel and Bell (1960) have shown, with considerable difficulties in helping to focus attention on the origins of the problem—often the marital inter-action. Parents produce characteristic defences to deal with their guilt over their treatment of the child : they see themselves as victims of the child; they emphasise how fortunate the child is materially; they interpret the child's disturbance as wilful badness.

Being the sick member of a family carries with it many secondary gains and may, as Parsons and Fox (1960) show, represent a passive withdrawal from normal activities and responsibilities—an escape from the pressures of ordinary life. Illness is a form of deviant behaviour which is partially and conditionally legitimised by society; a person is allowed to be ill and his failure to perform his usual roles is seen as not being his fault. Parsons and Fox lay great emphasis on the analogy of doctor and patient with parent and child, for in both cases a dependent relationship exists. The sick person is expected to accept his state as an undesirable one and is obliged to get well as soon as pos-sible. In the case of some forms of mental illness and personality disturbance, doctors and social workers find it difficult to tolerate the apparent resistance of the patient to treament and his failure to 'get better', and because he is 'unco-operative' his deviant behaviour is no longer tolerated. By analogy, the child is permitted to be 'childish' but is under an obligation to grow up.

The problem for the social worker is that of under-standing the impact of illness on the family members. Some families have an inherent tendency to set up a vicious circle of interaction which drives the sick person deeper and deeper into illness. This fact has important implictions for the development of a form of 'community care' for the mentally ill which may, in fact, mean primarily care by the patient's own family. In many socially and physically mobile families a great load is placed upon family relationships because of the relative isolation of the family and its lack of effective contact with the extended family. In these circumstances, roles within the family are very precariously distributed and the illness of one person, particularly if it is the mother, seriously disrupts the role distribution in the family.

The most interesting work that has been done recently on the sick role in the family is that of Laing and Esterson (1964) on the part played by the family in the genesis of schizophrenia. They suggest that social as well as genetic factors play a part in producing schizophrenia, and that the person who is diagnosed as schizophrenic is part of a wider network of extremely disturbed and disturbing patterns of communication within the family. With these patterns of communication, which involve the substitution of false for true interpretations of experience and motivation, one or more family members, usually parents, induce confusion in another family member, usually a child, as to his whole experience and actions. The 'victim' is given to understand that he feels happy or sad, regardless of his own perception of his emotion, and his motives and intentions are discounted or minimised and replaced by others. In this way the scapegoat becomes unsure of his own identity for he has to fit into a sterotyped role regardless of his own emotional needs. In such a schizogenic family there is a predominant absorption in fitting together family roles at the expense of recognising the individual differences and identities that actually exist. This 'psuedo-mutuality' (see Wynne, 1958) of family roles is maintained by coercion and manipulation, but because communication within the family is confused and distorted there is often an absence of overt conflict for the victim is in a 'can't win' situation of being unable to bring the conflict into the open and thus come to grips with it. The attempt to make the family all-inclusive will be successful until the scapegoat escapes from an intolerable situation into a schizophrenic breakdown.

## Socialisation and communication

Consideration of the distorted communications said to be characteristic of the families of schizophrenics points to the importance of communication generally in the socialisation of the child. Research of great significance to social work, especially that of Bernstein (1960, 1964, 1965) has been reported in recent years on the way in which different social structures generate different methods of communication.

Bernstein's hypothesis is that in lower working-class families the child learns a 'restricted' speech system which is appropriate to his natural environment but not for his relationships with middle-class institutions such as schools, psychiatric clinics and social work agencies. This restricted speech system, compared with the 'elaborated' speech system of the middle class, is characterised by a reduction in adjectives and adverbs, especially those which qualify feelings, and by an organisation of speech which is relatively simple, with little use of the pronoun 'I' and greater use of other personal pronouns. These differences in the speech systems of middle-class and working-class lie, Bernstein suggests, in differences between middle-class and working-class cultures. The restricted speech system is generated by certain kinds of social relationships charac- terised by common assumptions, shared interests and strong identification, a cultural identity which reduces the need to elaborate verbally an individual's intention and make it explicit. Such a speech system, where feelings are

61

taken for granted, is not necessarily class-linked but operates whenever social relationships are close, between friends, in peer groups of adolescents and children, and in closed communities such as prisons. The restricted speech system is available to and used by all members of society, but those in the lower working class are limited to this system and have no other.

It is the sociological and psycholigical implications of the restricted language system which are of particular relevance to social work. Unlike the elaborated speech system, the restricted system cannot easily be used to communicate unique experiences which emphasise separateness and difference, for this speech is concerned with expressing common interests and expectations—'us', and not with individual motivation and the special identity of 'I'. Uniqueness is expressed non-verbally rather than verbally, and whereas the bond of mother and child is very powerful in a non-verbal form the motivations and intentions of the mother and child are less available to each because less verbalised. Thus, the restricted system is a 'deprived language' which does not allow the individual to develop the ability to discriminate shades of meaning in the feelings and motivations of himself and others. This lack of perceptual discrimination shows itself in the characteristic ways in which middle-class and working-class parents exercise authority over their children. The appeals that are made by parents to children when attempting to control their behaviour are termed by Bernstein *person-orientated* and *status-orientated*. Person-orientated appeals are related to the *feelings* of the parent ('Mummy will be upset if you do that') and so elicit guilt in the child, or to the consequences of the child's actions, which allows for rational discussion. Status-orientated appeals rely for their effectiveness on the differences of status between parent and child, appeals which are essentially impersonal and transmit cultural norms in a very direct way. Punishment is usually quick to follow failure by a child to respond to such an appeal.

As we might expect, the lower working-class parent relies most upon the status-orientated appeal, and people brought up in this kind of cultural setting will have characteristic ways of dealing with anxiety. With a restricted speech system tensions are less subject to verbal control and will tend to be dissipated quickly through action. Lower working-class clients of social work agencies will tend to 'act-out' rather than 'talk-out' their problems, and their defence mechanisms will tend to be denial and displacement rather than rationalisation, the characteristic defence of the more verbally fluent middle-class social worker. The implications of all this for social work are considerable, as Nursten (1965) has shown, for they suggest the need for a complete re-examination of casework methods with lower working-class clients. These methods at present rely largely upon a form of verbal communication which may be culturally alien to those it is designed to help. Social workers, it seems, need to learn to communicate with some of their clients using a restricted language system with all that this assumes, and possibly with long term cases, to educate their clients into using and understanding a more elaborate language system.

### The influence of social class on child-rearing

Differences of speech and perception are but one facet of the correlation which exists between child-rearing and family organisation on the one hand, and social class on the other. A large number of studies of the social class correlates of child-rearing practices and the distribution of parental roles in the family have been undertaken in Britain and the United States, the British studies having been surveyed comprehensively in a two-volume work by Klein (1965). Here, we can merely indicate some aspects of the relationship between social class and socialisation which are of particular importance to the social worker.

In spite of the rapid social changes which are blurring class lines, most studies have suggested that the working-class family system is rigid, hierarchical and geared to the maintenance of order. Middle-class families, the studies suggest, tend to have more equalitarian relationships, and parental roles, as Bott (1957) found, are less differentiated and rigidly defined. Kohn (1960) in a study of parental authority, shows that middle-class mothers tend to emphasise the fathers' supportive role, whereas working-class mothers emphasise fathers' directive and constraining role. The difference in the father's role in middle-class and working-class families has been noted in many studies. In the middle-class families the father is seen as a companion to his son as well as an authority figure, whereas in the working-class family the father often remains a rather punitive figure while the mother in fact carries a great deal of authority. McKinley (1964) suggests that the father loses authority in the lowest social class as a consequence of his social and occupational inadequacy, thus supporting the view of Titmuss (1958); this leads him to general hostility and a reduced emotional involvement in the life of his son. The lower the social class the more rigid and punitive the father. Class-linked differences in the exercise of authority appear to reflect different patterns of expectations and values, differences in what is punished and what overlooked. In another study by Kohn (1959 b.) working-class parents showed themselves to be concerned primarily with immediate consequences of a child's acts and to focus attention upon the act itself, wheras middle-class parents responded in terms of interpretaions of the child's intent and took account of the child's motives and feelings. This appears to support Bernstein's findings. Kohn (1959 a.) also shows considerable class-linked differences in the qualities which the parents seek in their children, for, as we have seen, high priority is given by parents to those qualities which are judged important to the child in terms of its future adult role. Thus, middle-class parents tend to emphasise internalised standards of conduct: honesty, self-control, curiosity for boys, and consideration for girls. Working-class parents, on the other hand, tend to emphasise qualities that assure 'respectability'; obedience, neatness and cleanliness.

There appears to be general agreement in the studies in this field that there is greater use of physical punishment by working-class than by middle-class parents. In an important American study of child-rearing practices (Sears, Maccoby and Levin, 1957) substantial differences were evident in the characteristic techniques of control, differences which again appear to support Bernstein's work. On the basis of the evidence collected a distinction was made between *love-orientated techniques of control* and *object-orientated techniques*. The former techniques included praise as means of reward and isolation and withdrawal of love as punishments. These were essentially guilt-producing techniques, and although compared with other techniques superficially they appear to be more 'lenient', in fact they were more compelling and effective. The object-orientated techniques included tangible rewards as incentives to good behaviour and the deprivation of privileges and the use of physical force as punishments. These techniques were more punitive and restrictive than the former ones and more often resorted to by working-class than by middle-class parents. A pronounced use of reasoning as a form of guidance for the child tended to occur more commonly among mothers who used love-orientated techniques.

65

*Social class and basic personality*

The enduring effects of these different kinds of social class experience upon personality development are difficult to establish in a rigorous way, but attempts have been made to do this in Britain using Kardiner's theory (see Chapter Two) of the relationship between the child-rearing practices and basic personality type. Most notable is the study by Kerr (1958) of Liverpool slum families, which revealed a basic personality which the author saw as springing from the child-rearing disciplines and family structure of the sub-culture in which they lived. Three characteristics of these families stand out as significant: the feeding, the physical affection shown, and the authority of the mother. In these families the baby was normally breast-fed for a short period, and feeding was not seen as a time of affection, but as another job which mother had to do. Babies were fed when they cried, and the habit of feeding on demand rather than at set meal times continued as the child grew up. Informal demand feeding was characteristic throughout, with children helping themselves continuously to bread and margarine which they ate standing up. Working members of the family were also fed on demand and expected food immediately upon their return home from work. Food fads were very common among all the members of the family. Physical demonstrations of affection were common in these families, with the young baby often sleeping with mother and children preferring to sleep together in the same bed rather than in separate beds or separate rooms. The result of this close physical intimacy was to make adults often frightened of sleeping in rooms by themselves, but it appeared to help to cement family ties.

The most marked characteristic of the families which

Kerr studied was the dominant authority of the mother, maintained by a mixture of indulgence and threats. Shouting and violence was a frequent result of this dominance. The very strong maternal tie with the children had, Kerr maintains certain results so far as the personality traits of the children were concerned which continued into adulthood. Primary among these was an emotional insecurity which produced an attitude of reliance and dependence and an inability to take responsibilty. The emotional immaturity produced by over-dependence on mother resulted in violence, and an inability to plan. In such a mother-dominated culture, the boys tend to identify with mother rather than father, since father has little social status either inside the house or outside in the occupational world. Identification with mother solves the son's difficulties in trying to play a male role in a predominantly female society. Mothers appear to do as they wish, from a child's point of view, so by identifying with her he imagines that he will be able to do the same. The child grows up in fact, with a picture of an all-powerful, all-encompassing mother who is responsible for him and to whom he is responsible for his actions. The mother sets the moral code for the child, a code which is bound to be limited because the mother's social contacts are limited.

Spinley (1953) like Kerr, based her work upon Kardiner's theories and compared in terms of personality, a group of individuals who had received public school education with a group of slum dwellers. The major aim was to test the hypothesis that 'in treating two social groups which have very dissimilar environments, both material and social, two distinct ways of life are being studied with different "typical" personality structures'. Considerable contrasts (together with some similarities) existed between personality profiles of the public school group and the slum group. For example, the public school profile included the following: 'The individual has a strict, effective conscience; he faced disturbing situations and attempts to deal adequately with them. Present satisfactions are postponed for the sake of greater ones in the future.' For the slum group we have the following description: 'The individual shows marked absence of a strict and efficient conscience and unwillingness and inability to deal with disturbing or unpleasant situations and a flight from these. He is unable to postpone satisfactions.' Spinley's work, like Kerr's, is based largely upon inference, for strict *causal* relationships between child-rearing practices and personality structure are very difficult to establish.

One way out of the difficulty of establishing causal relationships is to study, as Miller and Swanson (1960), more precisely defined facets of personality rather than the all-embracing 'personality type'. Miller and Swanson attempted to test the hypothesis 'that differences in children's ways of resolving conflict reflect the contrasting experiences of social class'. They examined the characteristically preferred defences of middle-class and working-class children, and found that the former used defences which required many skills, involved minimal distortion, were specific to a situation and resulted in socially acceptable behaviour. Working-class children inclined to the use of defences requiring little previous experience, maximum distortion (for example denial and displacement) and creating social difficulties.

*Education and social class*

In spite of increased social mobility and the fact that the upper strata of the working class are increasingly developing middle-class attitudes and aspirations, it remains true that for the lower strata of the working class a distinctive
68

cultural heritage places them at a disadvantage in the educational system. Much evidence has been produced in recent years on differential opportunities in education, and particular mention should be made of the work of Floud *et. al.* (1956), Halsey *et. al.* (1962), Jackson and Marsden (1962) and Riessman (1962). By referring to Bernstein's work we can see immediately that lack of verbal ability is likely to be a severe handicap to a lower working-class child at school, a handicap which is revealed in the severely depressed verbal I.Q. scores of working-class compared with middle-class children. This, and the total cultural milieu of the lower working-class child, produces a difference in attitude to school itself compared with the middle-class child.

> Whereas the middle-class child learns a socially adaptive fear of receiving poor grades at school, of being aggressive towards the teacher, of fighting, of cursing, and of having early sexual relationships, the slum child learns to fear quite different social acts. His gang teaches him to fear being taken in by the teacher, of being a softie with her. To study homework seriously is literally a disgrace. Instead of boasting of good marks at school, one conceals them, if he ever receives any. (Davis, 1949)

This sense of separation from the middle-class culture of the school is reinforced continuously, as Jackson and Marsden and Mays (1962) have shown, by the indifference and hostility to education which characterises certain lower working-class communities.

From the very beginning of his school career the middle-class and lower working-class child may be expected to react differently to the discipline and restraint imposed upon him by school attendance. The middle-class child is

69

carefully prepared for the role of the school child. His parents expect achievement and convey to the child explicitly that he must do well at school if he wishes to maintain social status, and achieve a 'suitable occupation'. Green (1958) maintains that because the middle-class boy is more closely supervised by his mother than is the working-class boy, the former undergoes a 'personality absorption' which creates a dependence on adult authority much greater than the less well supervised lower working-class boy and makes him more prepared to co-operate with school teachers. Green produces no evidence to support his hypothesis of 'personality absorption', but what seems clear is that the middle-class child thrives on competition, a reflection of the middle-class occupational world, whereas the lower working-class child is more concerned perhaps, with solidarity, group allegiance, 'us' rather than 'I'. Intellectual ability and general 'brightness' shown by the child is rewarded in both the middle-class home and at school. In lower working-class homes rewards are given for quite different attributes because a different normative pattern governs the roles in the family. Looked at in terms of social learning, we can see that parents *reinforce* favourable responses in the child, 'favourable' being culturally defined in accordance with class norms, and this reinforcement is increased by success. Parents also *inhibit* unfavourable responses. Lower working-class attitudes towards education, however, cannot be dismissed as totally irrational, for they have to be seen within the context of the relative socio-economic deprivation of this strata of society. The lower working-class parent and child have no reason to assume that the value of education is self-evident, for the lower working-class occupational and cultural life does not allow for the essentially middle-class values enshrined in education. For lower working-class people the opportunities for social mobility are negligible and the school is the symbol of a competition in which they do not believe they can succeed.

What is likely to be the effect on the school-teacher of the presence of representatives of lower working-class sub-culture in the school? Through upbringing or subsequent social mobility via education, school-teachers, like social workers, are governed in their behaviour and attitudes by a middle-class value system. This may sometimes have the effect of leading them to penalise children who do not exhibit middle-class traits of cleanliness, punctuality and neatness, and instead exhibit uninhibited aggression. Thus, lower working-class children may feel rejected by their teachers and show a good deal of evident or hidden resentment because of this. Teachers may naturally feel that lower working-class children are deliberately defying them, whereas in fact the child-rearing practices of their culture provide a pattern of behaviour which is inconsistent with middle-class demands. The lower working-class child's resentment and feeling of separation prevents co-operation with the teacher in learning, and, therefore, provides a limitation on the development of the inherent ability of the child. In this way occupational advance and social mobility remain closed to such children, especially in a society which increasingly demands that a 'diploma *élite*' should occupy all responsible positions in the occupational hierarchy. It is self evident that social workers as much as teachers must understand and take full account of the social class factors which may operate in the educational attainments of children.

*Cultural values and social work*

In drawing together the implications for social work practice of the preceding material, one is struck immediately by the all-pervasive influence of cultural values on social diagnosis, methods of treatment and communication, and on the goals of social work. As a starting-point we may turn once again to the sociological view of social work as a mechanism of social control (see Taylor, 1958; Weisman and Chwast, 1960; Leonard, 1965). The processes by which society secures conformity to its expectations, include both *coercion* which emanates from the agencies of law and government and is accomplished by force or the threatened use of force, and by *persuasion* which operates to induce an individual to respond to the norms of the larger social group. Social work agencies may exercise various admixtures of coercion and persuasion, depending on their statutory powers, but all agencies, even those whose powers appear to be entirely persuasive, are concerned with the modification of human behaviour in the direction of certain cultural norms. Such a view of social work requires serious re-examination of the 'principle of client self-determination' and greater awareness of the power of the social worker in his relationship with the client. Control is subtly exercised by the social worker: the client may be induced to modify his behaviour because he requires what the social worker has to give, such as her skill and her power to change the environment. Evidence supporting this view may be found in the work of Dollard and Miller (1950) on psychological reinforcement. From this work we can suggest that the social worker reinforces by verbal or non-verbal communication certain kinds of responses and inhibits others, thus exercising control over the behaviour of the client. This view of the relationship between the social worker and the client stands in marked contrast to the view of many social work writers. Thus Davison (1965) writes: 'To assume that we know what is right for a client may be presumptious . . . the discovery for themselves, with the caseworker's help, of their right (*sic*) course of action is a very different

72

matter.' The distinction suggested in this statement may owe more to belief than to evidence, for the whole of social work is pervaded with concepts such as 'maladjusted', 'deviant', 'abnormal', 'neurotic', which are the modern judgemental equivalents of the older concepts 'good', 'bad', 'deserving' and 'undeserving'.

In looking at the relationship between cultural values and social work it is clearly essential to consider the particular cultural values of the *social worker* as well as the cultural values of the *client*. There is a tendency to assume, unthinkingly, that the social worker's values are in the last resort more *right* or more *natural*. The problems which may arise over a clash of values between the social worker and the client can be illustrated by considering the implications of different class attitudes to child-rearing and parental roles. These attitudes are important to social workers especially in connection with the current concept of the 'parental role' of the caseworker in his relationship with certain clients. Apart from the fact that the child care officer acts *in loco parentis* with regard to children in care, it is today commonly accepted that when working with immature and deprived clients the social worker may take on the role of a substitute parent. Thus Irvine (1964) suggests that in working with certain immature clients the caseworker needs to use authority, give advice and set limits and that 'in this type of casework the essential process lies in the acting-out of a parent-child relationship between worker and client'. The difficulty here is that the client's expectations as to the behaviour appropriate to a parental relationship will, as we have seen previously, depend in part upon his social class position. The social worker's and the client's expectations of the parental relationship may thus diverge not simply because of the client's psychopathology, but because of the conflict be-

F

tween the social worker's and client's cultural definitions of the parent-child relationship.

Divergence of values is most noticeable in the field of parental control over children's behaviour. As we have seen, the norms governing techniques and aims of parental control appear to be strongly class-linked. The implications of this divergence can be seen in an interview which took place between a family caseworker and a lower working-class mother who had beaten her young son quite severely because of his sexual curiosity. The caseworker in this interview was obviously very upset and failed to recognise that physical punishment was a totally acceptable form of parental control in that particular cultural milieu. She was mistaken in expecting the mother to feel remorse for the beating she had given, and wasting her time in trying to suggest to the mother that she must 'feel guilty'. In this same interview the caseworker felt obliged to suggest to the mother that the latter should 'talk things over' with her son, a suggestion which was culturally alien to the mother, though quite natural to the intellectual, highly verbal, middle-class social worker.

Here as elsewhere, the crucial diagnostic factor which the social worker has to take into account is the extent to which the client's problems are the result of a personality structure which has evolved from unique responses to personal life history, and the extent to which they reflect cultural conditioning. It is important for both assessment and treatment that the social worker should try to determine the balance of these factors, because if what social workers see as 'problems' are in fact culturally determined and supported by group norms, then there is less likelihood that those 'problems' will produce internal conflict in the client.

Emphasis on the culturally-laden values and expectations of social worker and client does not itself imply complete cultural relativism in social work, but that *awareness* of cultural differences is important for effective social work practice. The fact that a social worker's values are largely middle class in origin does not in itself condemn them, but it does demand care in making decisions which imply the superiority of one value over another. It may be argued that social workers have a function in society to help to accelerate adaptation to social change in the direction of values which encourage a higher mobility and less investment in extended family relationships. Society may be changing more rapidly than the life patterns of individuals and so social workers may feel justified in requiring from their lower working-class families greater joint flexibility of parental roles as these families themselves become more physically mobile and less matrilocal.

If we turn from the goals of social work to methods of treatment we can call upon the growing body of evidence in the psychiatric field that 'what happens therapeutically to a person who becomes a psychiatric patient is, to a significant degree, a function of his social class position in the community' (Schaffer and Myers, 1959). Space does not permit a review of this evidence, among which the New Haven study by Hollingshead and Redlich (1958) and the recent collection of research material by Riessman *et. al.* (1964) are the most notable. The American evidence suggests that lower working-class patients arc unable to make effective use of psychotherapy and that therapists tend to prefer to treat middle-class and skilled working-class patients. One might suggest that a similar problem faces the social worker concerned with lower working-class clients especially if the casework methods are largely modelled on psychotherapy. As we have seen, the problem here is likely to have its origins in class-linked differences of values, perception, and means of communication. If psychotherapy and insight-promoting casework techniques are less productive with lower working-class than with middle-class clients what conclusions should be drawn? One suggestion may be that these methods should be confined entirely to middle-class clientele. Thus Reusch (1964) maintains that 'the present methods of individual psychotherapy . . . are methods which were designed for use between people who belong approximately to the same social class and who share in common a large number of assumptions'. Another view may be that psychotherapy and casework are methods potentially adaptable to a wide range of individuals from different cultural origins and that the practitioners in these fields must strive to adapt their techniques to make them more widely effective.

# 4

# The analysis of social work organisations

In Chapter Two we examined the way sociologists approach the study of social groups in terms of the roles and values governing the interaction of group members. As an example of this approach we referred to interaction between members of a particular kind of group—the social work agency. In this chapter we shall indicate the main lines of a sociological approach to the study of the organisation of social work, with particular attention to the special problems of large-scale social work organisations. The social group for which the term *organisation* is used is that which pursues specific goals and is characterised by division of labour and the existence of a hierarchy. Organisations, particularly large-scale ones, are an ever present part of modern industrial society and abound in economic, political, religious, educational and social service fields.

## Scientific management

Scientific interest in the nature of organisations and the effect of group interaction within them began in the industrial and business sphere. The motivation for the study of business organisations came from the desire to find ways of increasing efficiency and productivity and led to the

'Scientific Management' approach of F. W. Taylor and his followers, dominant in the early decades of this century (Taylor, 1911). This approach, following the classical view of 'economic man', stressed the essential rationality of the behaviour of men in organisations. Workers were seen as motivated basically by economic rewards, so that if material rewards were closely related to work efforts, the worker would respond with the maximum performance of which he was capable. 'Time-and-motion' study, the interest of management in piece-work wages and economic incentives for workers, and the use of 'efficiency experts' in industrial concerns, all stem from a 'Scientific Management' approach, which has tended at times to view the industrial worker as an appendage of the factory machine. The emphasis on rationality in the 'Scientific Management' approach led to concentration on division of labour and an extolling of the virtues of assembly-line production.

It was at a time when, in the United States, interest in industrial organisation centred on the physiological aspects of efficiency, that Elton Mayo, a psychologist and two engineers Roethlisberger and Whitehead, began a series of famous studies of the Hawthorne Works of the Western Electric Company. Contrary to the expectations that the 'Scientific Management' approach suggested, they found that it was not better lighting, cash bonuses or rest pauses that increased the workers' morale, and therefore their productivity, but the fact that for the purposes of the study they were no longer isolated as individuals but were working together in groups. The Hawthorne studies (Roethlisberger and Dickson, 1939) demonstrated conclusively that there was not, as was previously thought, a simple and direct relationship between physical working conditions and the rate of production. Specifically, the study showed that the level of production was set by the social norms of the group rather than by physiological capacities, and that non-economic rewards and sanctions determined by the group itself were more important than economic bonuses. In general terms, the studies revealed that workers do not act as individuals, but as members of groups.

## Human relations in industry

The Hawthorne studies marked the beginning of the Human Relations approach to the worker in industry, an approach propagated with much fervour by Elton Mayo and embraced with enthusiasm by management in the United States and eventually in Britain also. Mayo summarised his views in the following terms: 'The need for appreciation, security and familiar company is more important as a factor in labour morale than wages and physical conditions' (Mayo, 1949). Such an approach, with its concentration upon the non-rational elements in organisational behaviour, was in marked contrast to the 'Scientific Management' approach, but could nevertheless develop into a managerial sociology which emphasised 'human relations' and ignored economic realities. The Human Relations view suggests that by social engineering the manager may produce a situation in which conflict of interests between workers and management no longer exists, for, contrary to the Marxist thesis, such conflict is not inevitable but may be managed away by careful consideration of the human needs of workers. Such consideration of the workers' needs will have the long-run effect of fulfilling the manager's goals also—the maximisation of profit. Gardner envisages the possibility of complete identification of the worker with the organisation which employs him:

employees should have a feeling that the company's goal is worth their effort; they should feel themselves part of the company and take pride in their contribution to its goal. This means that the company's objectives must

79

be such as to inspire confidence in the intentions of management and belief that each will get rewards and satisfactions by working for these objectives. (Gardner, 1945)

The derisive laughter with which most factory workers would be likely to greet Gardner's statement points to an important weakness in the Human Relations approach to organisational behaviour—its failure to recognise that conflict between management and labour is endemic in mass-production industry because the management's objectives in rationalising production alienate the worker (Chinoy, 1955). Such conflict may be institutionalised and made less disruptive through the existence of trade unions and consultative machinery, but it remains conflict. In spite of their limitations, both scientific management and human relations approaches have made valuable contributions to the understanding of organisations, the former view emphasising the *formal* aspects of organisation (the organisational pattern as laid down by management) whilst the latter view has highlighted the *informal* aspects (the social relations which develop in organisations).

*The structuralist approach*

Building upon the insights of the two previous approaches, the Structuralist school, rooted in the work of Weber and Marx, has been able to take account of both formal and informal aspects of organisation and provides an analysis which admits to the reality of a conflict of interests and so avoids the taint of a managerial sociology. A structuralist approach is now adopted by most students of organisation for it provides a more all-inclusive framework for study than did previous schools, and is applied to a wide range of organisations other than business and economic ones. Simon (1961) primarily a student of the formal rational aspects of organisation, takes this wider view when considering the processes of decision-making in organisations:

> . . . *organisation* refers to the complex pattern of communications and other relations in a group of human beings. This pattern provides to each member of the group much of the information, assumptions, goals, and attitudes that enter into his decisions, and provides him also with a set of stable and comprehensible expectations as to what the other members of the group are doing and how they will react to what he says and does.

## Bureaucracy

As organisations increase in size and complexity they face characteristic problems. Direction, co-ordination and communication become more difficult and the amount of internal administration increases. Informal methods of communication and administration become increasingly inappropriate, and more formal, rational patterns of interaction are necessary. Thus, large-scale organisations develop *bureaucracy* as a means of coping with increased size and complexity. The term 'bureaucracy' is used popularly to denote 'officialdom', 'red tape' and other undesirable aspects of large-scale administration, but sociologically the term does not imply a value judgement. It simply refers to the rational and clearly defined arrangement of activities which are directed towards fulfilling the purposes of the organisation. Bureaucracies have, Max Weber (1947) maintained, certain interrelated characteristics which contribute to their maintenance and efficiency. These characteristics include a clearly defined hierarchy of offices or positions, each of which carries particular responsibilities and authority, the selection of candidates on the basis of technical qualifications, the existence of a body of rules and regulations which govern the performance of official roles, and a career structure which involves security of tenure provided these roles are performed efficiently.

## Bureaucracy in social work

Social work is now undertaken primarily in organisations marked by specialisation and hierarchy, having specific functions laid down by Act of Parliament and supplemented by rules and regulations which govern the goals and methods of the social worker in relation to his client. Increasingly, the social work agency provides a career structure which may allow for rapid promotion to supervisory grades; this applies especially to a situation of acute shortage of staff, for example in the child care service. The supervision of lower grades is an essential requirement of bureaucracy, but in the case of social work it coincides with a belief in the educational value of supervision.

The process of supervision in social work has aroused some interest amongst sociologists concerned with social work organisation. Suggestions have been made that supervision, because it is often conceived in educational and pseudo-therapeutic terms, is in fact a means of subtle manipulation. It is maintained that social workers use a Human Relations technique for controlling students and subordinates in the organisation because they are reluctant to use direct authority. Such supervisors concentrate upon the personality characteristics of the subordinate rather than his work performance. Wilensky and Lebeaux (1958) write:

> Since sensitivity to the motivational and emotional states of the client—perhaps the prime objective of social work training—must be preceded by self-awareness, the student is himself subjected to a near psychotherapeutic experience. He is persistently called to account for his

own behaviour, not in cognitive but in emotional terms
—not 'Why do you think this way?' but 'Why do you
feel this way?'

Blau and Scott (1963), reporting on a study of a social work
agency, show that what appears to be democratic in supervision may be merely manipulative:

> Workers whose judgement frequently differed from that
> of their supervisors might be accused of being 'unable
> to accept supervision'. The practice of questioning the
> worker's unconscious motives tended to elevate the
> superordinate into an omniscient power. Workers found
> that they could not be right in any disagreement since
> their arguments were not accepted at their face value
> but dismissed as being rationalisations to mask uncon-
> scious resistance.

Such manipulative disregard of the *content* of communications from below may be characteristic of organisations
with therapeutic functions, for this phenomena was
detected by both Caudill (1958) and Stanton and Schwartz
(1954) in their studies of social interaction in psychiatric
hospitals.

Not all social work supervision is of this pseudo-
therapeutic kind, of course, and it may be more prominent
in American than in British social work. Within the
bureaucratic setting staff supervision has normally implied
control and the direct use of authority. Blau and Scott
were able to study the effects of authoritarian supervision
in their studies of two social work agencies. Authoritarian
supervision was defined as strict, close supervision with
rigid regard for procedures and regulations. The effects of
this style of supervision compared with other styles included a decrease in the social worker's satisfaction with
the job, the fostering of a narrow concern with client

eligibility rather than with client's needs more liberally interpreted, and a marked reluctance to assume responsibility. Such authoritarian supervisors were felt by their subordinates not to be casework orientated. Productivity, which Blau and Scott rather naïvely measured by the number of visits per month per social worker, was not related to authoritarian supervision, but no measure was obtained of the quality of the social work undertaken. The personal characteristic which social workers appreciated most in a supervisor was emotional detachment—not getting too excited or anxious about a case—and supervisors of this kind had social workers whose productivity was high.

## Bureaucracy and group interaction

The development of bureaucracy in social work has had both beneficial and harmful results, and in attempting to assess these the effects of informal group interaction have to be considered as well as the formal structure of the agency. As Donnison and Chapman (1965) demonstrate in a number of studies of organisational change, such studies must include an examination first of the formal organisational structure, second of the way the organisation works from the point of view of its members, and third, of the way the organisation works from the investigator's point of view.

One of the major effects of bureaucracy is sometimes referred to as 'the routinisation of activity' by which rules and regulations are laid down by the organisation and have to be followed, with a resulting emphasis upon client eligibility as defined by the rules. This is not a universal result, however, for the degree of emphasis on narrow eligibility will depend in part upon informal group interaction within the organisation. In Blau and Scott's study a distinction was made between social workers of the agency who were 'procedure orientated', concerned primarily with checking client eligibility, and those who were 'service orientated', aiming to provide a casework service for the client. Among workers with less than three years experience, more than half of the 'highly integrated' ones (who were popular and had informal group support) were 'service orientated', but less than a quarter of the 'unintegrated' workers (lacking group support and popularity) were. Among those social workers with over three years experience, the degree of group support did not appear to effect their orientation. This result suggests the importance of strong group support for new social workers in preventing their natural concern with unfamiliar procedures leading them to abandon the service orientated approach which they are likely to have been taught in their training.

When looking at group interaction in a social work agency one would expect to find, following the sociological theory expounded in Chapter Two, that the values governing the role performance of group members would affect the behaviour of members in the direction of conforming to group values. To test this hypothesis, Blau and Scott sought to discover how group attitudes affected members' conduct *regardless* of their own personal attitudes. To do this the investigators had to separate the effects of the external influence of group pressure from the internal influence of the individual's own personality, thus isolating the *structural* effects of the group on individual behaviour. By comparing the majority views among social workers in different sections of the same social work agency with the individual views within these sections, it was shown that if a 'service orientated' attitude prevails in a group, then the individual social worker who merely checks client eligibility experiences strong disapproval and a pressure to conform to group norms. The same pressure was exerted on those 'deviants' who were 'service orientated' but who belonged to a section which was predominantly 'procedure orientated'. The validity of these results is confirmed constantly by the experiences of newly-trained social workers entering agencies where group attitudes are predominantly hostile to social work training and the professional behaviour and attitudes which this training seeks to promote.

## Specialisation in social work

Specialisation of functions is a necessary part of bureaucratic organisation, for division of labour is essential in an advanced industrial society in order to increase efficiency and skill. In social work, the specialisation of functions between agencies has very clear advantages (see Winnicott, 1964) but also disadvantages. Titmuss (1954) points to the fact that the arrangement of social work tasks has tended to follow the administrative arrangement of the social services and that what was administratively appropriate or desirable in the past may be less desirable from the angle of people with needs. Specialisation between agencies may lead to rigidity and the development of agency sterotypes as to their own and other agencies' functions at a time when social change demands flexibility and the awareness of new needs (see Leonard, 1963).

Specifically, the effect of agency specialisation on the client is to require him to play a role reciprocal to that of the social worker in the agency and so present his problems in such a way as to fit in to the specialisation of the agency. Parents may feel that they have to approach the Children's Department with an overt request for the child to be admitted into care, whilst for the same problem they may have approached a Child Guidance Clinic with a request for treatment for the child, or a family casework agency for help with a marriage problem. The client, by his behaviour, has to *prove* that he needs the specific service which the agency provides, 'he must behave like a "case" if he is to use the service' (Wilensky and Lebeaux, 1958).

## The Professional in a bureaucracy

The effects of bureaucratic organisation on social work practice will be influenced to a considerable degree by the professionalism of the social workers themselves. There is evidence of strain and conflict within many organisations arising from the different orientations and allegiances of professionals and administrators, conflicts due in part to the different nature of professional and administrative authority. Etzioni (1964) writes:

> . . . the ultimate justification for a professional act is that it is, to the best of the professional's knowledge, the right act. He might consult his colleagues before he acts, but the decision is his. If he errs, he still will be defended by his peers. The ultimate justification of an administrative act, however, is that it is in line with the organisation's rules and regulations, and that it has been approved—directly or by implication—by a superior rank.

This fundamental difference of orientation appears to be common to all bureaucratic structures and accounts for the resistance of professionals, such as doctors and lawyers, to incorporation within such organisations. His specialised technical knowledge makes the professional an authority within a limited field, and he therefore does not need the sanctions of an organisation to support his professional decisions. The professional feels most at home in a group of equals, such as a professional association, and is less comfortable in the hierarchical structure which characterises bureaucracies. In spite of this resistance, however, many developments in society accelerate the pressure towards the bureaucratisation of the professions, leading to the large-scale impersonal organisation of their functions.

This view of the structural nature of the conflict between the administrator and the professional becomes complicated and modified when we apply it to social work because of the uncertain professional status of the social worker. Social workers are becoming increasingly sensitive about their professional status, and their uncertainty and insecurity remains evident. An American social work teacher demonstrates the heat which this subject generates:

> Social workers expend great effort trying to identify the characteristics that distinguish their profession from allied professions. On the one hand, they manifest an excess of deference in the company of physicians, psychiatrists, sociologists and anthropologists; on the other hand, they evince a narrow provincialism in their practice and in their education. This professional provincialism is offensive to other scholars and professionals and to the general public. All perceive the insecurity that underlies it. (Lutz, 1964)

In claiming professional status social workers are faced with the fact that untrained people perform the same tasks as professionally-trained social workers, for example in the fields of child care and probation. Thus, it is difficult for the professionally-trained social worker to produce evidence to show either superior knowledge or superior skill compared with the non-trained. For these and other reasons most sociologists have seen social work as a semi-profession and consequently more open to bureaucratisation. On the other hand, the more social work aspires to full professional status the greater will be the potential

88

conflict inherent in its inclusion in large-scale hierarchical organisations.

## Organisational loyalty

One of the major areas of potential conflict between administrator and social worker concerns loyalty to the organisation for whom both work, for there is evidence that unlike the administrator the professional feels loyalty primarily to the profession itself rather than to the organisation. Gouldner (1957) in a study of a small college, suggested that professionals lacked organisational loyalty and tended to be 'cosmopolitan', moving from one organisation to another, whereas those with less professional commitment had stronger organisational loyalty. Blau and Scott showed that there was a tendency for social workers with professional training to be orientated primarily to the profession itself and not to the social work agency. As social workers become more professional and owe allegiance to a body of principles and ethical standards which lie outside the organisational setting in which they work, they become less amenable 'organisation men' (Whyte, 1959). By providing a professional critique of the agency's methods and goals they present the administrator with considerable management problems.

Differences in organisational commitment represent but one aspect of a more fundamental difference in the goals typically pursued by the administrator and the social worker in the social services. The administrator is concerned with the maintenance of the organisation *as such*, even though he may be a professionally-trained social worker himself. As Wardell (1955) suggests, the administrator has responsibility for the decision-making necessary to co-ordinate an organisation *as a going concern*, and so a professional social worker who becomes the head of an agency must focus on goals different from those of the practitioner.

## Evaluation and decision-making

In the social services, administrators are primarily concerned with results, whereas the professional social worker may be primarily concerned with doing things in the proper professional manner and with results evaluated in a way different from that of the administrator. In a semi-profession such as social work there may arise through insecurity pressures towards 'professionally correct behaviour', often narrowly and rigidly defined. In some respects, the administrator together with the non-trained social worker may be more open-minded than the professional social worker who is unable to explore new ways of helping clients because of the parochialism which professional education and orientation may produce. The recent history of social work contains many examples of work being undertaken by some social workers, many of them untrained, which was dismissed by others as 'not professional' or 'not really casework'. Certain kinds of actions engaged in by the social worker such as the verbal interpretation of the client's behaviour, were accorded high social status within the profession, whereas other actions, such as the authoritative giving of advice, were accorded low status. Some social work writers have provided a retrospective theoretical justification for what was previously considered non-professional work. Irvine (1956) for example, suggested that the authoritative and supportive actions of social workers could be seen as 'role-playing' and as theoretically sound as the 'insight-promoting techniques' which received prominence in psychoanalytically-orientated casework literature.

The social worker's concern with professional behaviour

and with results defined in terms of the client's emotional as well as physical needs provides a potentially vital protection for the individual citizen involved in rigid and eligibility-based social services. Unfortunately, the social worker may be unable to resist narrowly conceived bureaucratic solutions to problems, as our previous discussion of the influence of group pressure shows.

A problem that all large-scale organisations face is that of what decisions are to be made at what point in the organisational hierarchy. The more professionally orientated the social worker becomes the more he will wish to have responsibility to make decisions which he considers to be within the area of his professional competence, rather than pass decisions upwards for executive action. In some social work organisations, such as Children's Departments, there is great difficulty in disentangling the legitimate interests of administrator and social worker in many areas of decision-making which involve far-reaching financial and administrative considerations. This can be seen particularly in the repercussions of the Children and Young Persons Act, 1963, which, among other things, gave local authorities power to grant financial and material aid to families in need. To what extent is the decision to give or withhold material aid a professional one ('Is it in the client's best interests?'), a legal one ('Is it within the terms of the Act?'), a financial one ('Is it within the limits laid down by the Finance Committee?') or a political one ('Will the ratepayers stand for it?')? Clearly, all these factors may be expected to play a part in such individual decision-making, and the conflicts will arise over the weighting and interpretation given to the various facts. The bureaucratic solution to this problem may be to deal with it as essentially an administrative matter, and in one of the largest Children's Departments in the country, all decisions about the giving of material and financial aid are made by one man, the chief officer. The extent to which social workers accept such a solution is, perhaps, in inverse ratio to the degree of their professional orientation.

## Bureaucracy and personality

In his *Bureaucratic Structure and Personality* (1957) Merton suggests that the personality characteristics of people in certain occupations emerge as a response to the distinctive structural pressures which are encountered in a particular job. In examining the 'dysfunctions' of bureaucracy Merton suggests that the pressures on employees in large-scale organisations induce them to engage in the sort of exaggerated behaviour which is popularly labelled 'bureaucratic'—a term used in this instance in a disparaging way. This view of bureaucratic behaviour supports the social worker's tendency to see conflict with the administrator in terms of the latter's personality, but relates it to structural factors operating in the organisation itself. If a large-scale social work organisation is to operate efficiently it must, as any other bureaucracy, attain a high degree of reliability in the behaviour of its staff so that they conform to the prescribed patterns and regulations laid down. With this in view it is natural that the head of any social work agency will want to inculcate attitudes in the staff which increase feelings of loyalty to the organisation itself. Career grading and promotion in a social work organisation may well come to depend, as in most bureaucracies, upon 'ability to accept authority' and a 'realistic understanding of the limitations of the job'. In this way the professional social worker's external point of reference may become a hindrance to promotion while the social worker who has been unable to resist the pressures of bureaucracy displaces his goals from ends to means and develops a characteristic rigidity.

92

# 5

# The future of sociology in social work

In the preceding chapters we have pointed to some of the theory and research in sociology which seems to be of relevance to the practice of social work. Of necessity, the space devoted to particular topics has been brief and intended merely to indicate the major lines of a sociological approach to problems of interest to the social worker. Also, some areas of sociology, such as those devoted to the study of delinquency and mental illness, have been omitted because they are to be the subject of other volumes in the companion series. We are, however, now in a position to draw together some of the issues which face social work in its effort to assimilate contributions from the field of sociology into the body of knowledge on which practice is based. We are also able to indicate those areas of sociological knowledge which seem at present to offer the most fruitful contributions.

## Science and values in sociology

Social work is developing as a professional discipline which, like sociology, is concerned with scientific validation but also, as we have seen, with certain values which lie embedded in the culture from which social work springs. Social work is interested in the discovery and interpretation of facts only in so far as they assist in *doing something* about social problems of individuals and groups. Should sociology likewise be directed towards social action? If it were directed exclusively towards the solving of social problems would it have greater relevance for social work? Such questions are important for social work for they highlight the special problems of borrowing knowledge from an academic discipline compared with borrowing from a body of theory derived from therapeutic endeavour, such as psychoanalysis.

This issue concerns the nature of sociology itself, its scientific status and its relation to values. Most sociologists would accept that the desire for a scientific basis for sociology is rooted in the status which science has in western industrial society and the high value which is placed upon scientific discovery. This does not make any judgement on the *validity* of science as a value, but simply recognises that the discipline of sociology itself must be seen against its cutural and historical background. However, beyond this there is disagreement among sociologists about how far the claims of sociology to be a science are justified, and whether it can be divorced from value-judgements.

Some sociologists stress the 'natural' character of human behaviour and the possibility of developing research methods comparable with those of the 'natural sciences'. These research methods would be directed towards the building up of a body of sociological principles which could be universally applied, methods which would comprise rigorous experimental techniques excluding all phenomena which could not be observed directly. Parsons (1937) and his colleagues, in developing a general theory of action, have striven for universality but at the same time have been prepared to include in their theory nonobservable phenomena such as motives, values, etc. The controversy as to what research methods are legitimate if sociology is to be called a science rests upon the minimum level of verifiability that any statement must have if it is to be regarded as a scientific statement. Sociologists have taken different approaches to this matter. One approach has been to use any method of research which promises to result in generalisations superior to common sense, the method being determined by the nature of the social phenomena being observed and the kind of technique available at the time. Other sociologists have insisted upon strict experimental method and the limitation of research to social phenomena which can be studied in this rigorous way.

To the social worker the importance of these differences of approach lies primarily in the amount of confidence he can have in research results, and whether they concern problems in which he is interested, problems which may present serious methodological difficulties to the investigating sociologist.

The issue concerning values in sociology has been that of the influence of the sociologist's own values on his work. While most sociologists would accept the objectivity of values as phenomena which influence human beings, they would regard the objective *validity* of values as a problem which lies outside sociology as a science—a problem for the philosopher and the theologian. Thus, Durkheim (1897) eschewed political commitment in the sociologist: 'Sociology . . . will be neither individualistic, Communistic, nor socialistic . . . On principle it will ignore these theories, in which it could not recognise any scientific value, since they tend not to describe or interpret, but to reform, social organisation.' Many sociologists, following Durkheim and Weber, have insisted that the social sciences must be value-free in the sense that the value commitments of the social scientist should play no role in the analysis of social data. Others, including Simey (1964) in Britain and the followers of C. Wright Mills in the United States, have reservations about the desirability or possibility of a value-free sociology:

> It would seem that social science's affinity for modelling itself after physical science might lead to instruction in matters other than research alone. Before Hiroshima, physicists also talked of a value-free science; they, too, vowed to make no value-judgements. Today many of them are not so sure . . . Granted that science always has inherent in it both constructive and destructive potentialities, it does not follow that we should encourage our students to be oblivious of the difference. (Gouldner, 1964)

Weber himself saw that freedom from value-judgements by the sociologist was only possible to a limited degree in that ultimate values would direct the sociologist to determine the kind of problem he was interested in, the assumptions built into his fundamental theoretical conceptions, and the range of data he would investigate.

Controversy over the ethical commitment of the sociologist arises in relation to the status of 'social administration' as a branch of sociology. The work of Titmuss and Townsend, for example, is sometimes questioned on the grounds that their obvious political views leads them to produce concrete proposals for administrative action for the amelioration of social problems. Some sociologists would hold that such proposals have no place in a sociologist's research report and that whatever facts emerge from research should be allowed to speak for themselves. From the social worker's point of view the major consideration in this controversy is whether social and ethical commitment is likely to distort to any considerable degree the research findings of sociologists concerned with social problems and the social services. There is, of course, no agreement as to whether this is so, but clearly in sociology as in social work the *facts* must be established in as scientific a manner as possible, and effort made to ensure that value judgements are made *explicit*, rather than hidden. The social worker is interested in therapeutically or diagnostically 'useful' results from sociological research, but such results can come from any number of sociological approaches, 'ethically committed' or otherwise. Sociology which devotes attention exclusively to social problems is not the only kind from which social work may benefit.

## The assimilation of sociological knowledge

Although social work can usefully call upon sociological theory and research to assist in understanding and helping with individual and group problems, the task of assimilating sociological knowledge presents certain difficulties (see Kadushin, 1959). Having become familiar with the vocabularies of psychology and psychiatry, social workers have to learn another set of concepts with a different focus. The social worker has to move back and forth in the analysis of problems between two distinct frames of reference— personality on the one hand and social interaction on the other—and this itself makes considerable intellectual demands (see Devereux, 1963).

The social worker, because he is primarily interested in specific applications of knowledge is usually more at home with the individual approach of psychology than with the wider generalisations of sociology. Sociologists attempt to apply the canons of scientific method to the evaluation of the results of any piece of research, while social workers are, by the very nature of their job, obliged to be 'opportunists' eager to use 'helpful' hypotheses, without too much concern for the evidence supporting them. Social workers cannot wait until a hypothesis is verified by substantial research because they have to continue to do their work and use whatever hypotheses and speculations are available to them. This does not excuse social workers, however, from trying to be aware of the scientific status of the concepts they are using—whether these concepts derive from well-substantiated theory, hypotheses in the process of being validated, or imaginative speculations.

The danger which social work faces here is that it may endow the knowledge which it borrows from sociology with greater certainty, and with greater simplicity, than would the sociologist. Social work has tended to do this in the past with regard to psychoanalysis, where speculation has often been received as fact. There were some unfortunate results in the field of social work from the over-eager acceptance of a grossly simplified version of Bowlby's hypothesis on the effects of maternal separation. Sociological propositions similarily need to be treated with caution, to be questioned as to the evidence which supports them, and to be placed within a framework which takes into account the whole man, biological, psychological and social. How are social workers to determine, from the vast corpus of sociological material, what is likely to be of use to them? (see Hollis, 1959). Clearly they themselves must decide what is to be used. It is the responsibility of social work teachers, for instance, to incorporate sociological knowledge into their teaching of social work practice, rather than relying entirely upon professional sociologists to provide courses for their students. Social workers must test out for themselves whether sociological hypotheses offer new, more convincing, better substantiated or more economical explanations of human behaviour than those provided by the hypotheses which social workers already use. For example, the description of social interaction derived from role theory, such as that of Spiegel (1960) referred to in Chapter Three, though it may provide a diagnostically useful framework for the social worker if used with care, may also deteriorate into a pompous and wordy formulation of a few simple and obvious ideas, as Andreski (1964) suggests. Banton (1964) admits that the term 'role' suffers from 'conceptual inflation' but maintains that it is nevertheless of great potential use. The value of role theory in social work will to a large extent be dependent upon preventing its being used as a jargon-laden substitute for the careful examination of social interaction.

Because social workers adopt a multidimensional approach to the understanding of individuals in society, they need to be as cautious in examining the concepts of sociological determinists as they would be in examining the ideas of biological determinism. The tendency of some sociological theory, as we saw in Chapter Two, is to suggest that personality is almost entirely the result of environmental conditioning, an 'oversocialised view of man' (Wrong, 1961) which underestimates the importance of biological drives. In using sociological knowledge social workers will be careful not to modify or abandon existing concepts before the full implications of the new ones are explored. For example, the 'over-socialised' conception of man of the dominant sociological schools places emphasis upon order and stability and pictures man as infinitely plastic in the face of cultural pressures—an approach which needs to be set against the Freudian recognition of conflict between instincts and socialisation:

To Freud man is a *social* animal without being entirely a *socialised* animal. His very social nature is the source of conflicts and antagonisms that create resistance to socialisation by the norms of any of the societies which have existed in the course of human history . . . All cultures, as Freud contended, do violence to man's socialised bodily drives, but this in no sense means that men could possibly exist without culture or independent of society. (Wrong, 1961)

## The future use of sociological knowledge

Bearing in mind the problems of assimilation, we can outline the major areas of sociological knowledge from which the most fruitful contributions to social work are likely to come in the future. Each of these closely related areas gives rise to numerous questions which social workers will wish to ask themselves and which they may wish to answer by research (see Kahn, 1957).

The *first* of these areas covers the data which social workers need in order to understand the client in the context of his socio-cultural background: the influence of family, social class and total culture on his attitudes to his problems and to the services and skill which the social worker offers. Some of the major questions are:

1. What is the effect of particular cultural settings on the expectations, goals, perceptions and evaluations of both clients and social workers?
2. What are the socio-cultural factors which effect the sexual identification of clients and their view of marital and parental roles?
3. What are the effects of clients' occupations on their roles as parents?
4. What are the social factors which determine a family's ability to contain and cope with internal crises, such as illness? Why do some families use the social services in these circumstances and others not?

5. To what extent does a client's verbal ability affect the social work treatment he receives and do the results of treatment depend upon the client's ability or willingness to communicate his feelings verbally?

The *second* area of social work interest to which sociology may make contributions is the development of theoretical concepts to help understand the social interaction between clients, the environment and the social worker. The questions we have to ask here include:

1. What are the theories, hypotheses and speculations which social workers *actually* use in their day-to-day work with clients, and how do these compare with the theory presented in social work text-books?
2. To what extent would it be possible to develop distinctive typologies of social problems for use in social work which would supplement psychiatric classification? (see Voiland *et al.*, 1962).
3. Can sociological concepts of social interaction be integrated with concepts from different frames of reference, such as those of the schools of psychology (e.g. psychoanalysis and learning theory) to produce more complete psychosocial theories of causation for use in social work?

The *third* area social workers may explore with the aid of sociology is the formal and informal organisation of social work agencies and the effect of such organisation on social work practice. This exploration would attempt to answer such questions as:

1. What are the organisational factors which influence social work practice and in particular decision-making?
2. What is the relationship between committee members,

administrators and social workers in local authority departments?

3. Does professional training affect the orientation and actual behaviour of social workers in relation to the agency, colleagues and clients? Does orientation and behaviour change over time?

4. How do social workers view their agency's function and do their views affect their expectations, perceptions and evaluation of clients and their problems?

## Conclusion

Sociology has much to offer social work, not least in its insistence upon the need for research in order to develop and test hypotheses about human behaviour. Social work cannot long continue to depend for its knowledge predominantly upon research undertaken and theory developed in other disciplines. The teaching of social work cannot remain linked almost entirely to the discussion of individual cases, but must be based increasingly upon research into social work practice which is designed to discover the elements which go to make up the skills which the social worker in an agency develops to help clients. Social work must extend its own research into the problems and characteristics of its clients. In these tasks, sociology, along with other branches of knowledge, will make an important contribution.

# 6

# Guide to the literature

Apart from R. M. McIver's *The Contribution of Sociology to Social Work* (Columbia University Press, 1931) there is no other single volume which deals exclusively with the subject matter of this book. The reader who wishes to examine further the relationship between sociology and social work must therefore be prepared to undertake fairly extensive reading from a number of sources, many of which have already been quoted in the text. Before looking at the literature relevant to the major themes of this book we shall comment on reading which covers sociology generally.

## General reading

H. D. Stein and R. A. Cloward (Eds.), *Social Perspectives on Behaviour* (Glencoe, The Free Press, 1961) is a useful collection of articles in the field of sociology and anthropology specially selected for their relevance to social work. Another American collection of articles on the interaction between personality and society is N. J. and W. T. Smelser, *Personality and Social Systems* (New York, Wiley, 1963). Part Six of this book examines the relationship between social structures and therapy, including social work, and all the articles are linked by editorial comment of particular theoretical clarity and logical rigour.

General text-books on sociology are legion, the vast majority being American. Of these, Ely Chinoy, *Society, An Introduction to Sociology* (New York, Random House, 1964) is a recent introductory text which is easy to read, covering the fields of sociology and examining wider philosophical issues. A more advanced text-book, firmly wedded to the structural-functional school is H. M. Johnson, *Sociology: A Systematic Introduction* (London, Routledge and Kegan Paul, 1961). A series of brief paper-back introductions to the various fields of sociology are being produced by Prentice-Hall Inc. under the general title 'Foundations of Modern Sociology Series'. The first volume of this series, written by the editor, is Alex Inkeles, *What is Sociology?* (New Jersey, Prentice-Hall, 1964) a very concise statement which orientates the reader to the whole field of sociology.

The most useful recent British introduction to sociology is T. B. Bottomore, *Sociology: A Guide to Problems and Literature* (London, Allen and Unwin, 1962) and published in a paper-back edition. Although written with special reference to Indian society, it covers for the general reader the major sociological concepts, theories and methods and provides useful notes on further reading. S. Andreski, *Elements of Comparative Sociology* (London, Weidenfeld and Nicholson, 1964) covers a number of theoretical and methodological issues in an astringent manner, and T. H. Marshall, *Sociology at the Crossroads* (London, Heinemann, 1963) is a collection of essays which includes the well-known 'Citizenship and Social Class'. On the history of sociology see H. Maus, *A Short History of Sociology* (London, Routledge and Kegan Paul, 1962), a brief survey of major developments in European and American sociology. John Madge, *The Origins of Scientific Sociology* (London,

Tavistock Publications, 1963) provides an account and critique of some major works in the recent history of sociology, including those of Durkheim, Thomas and Znanieki, Park and the Chicago school and later sociologists. The British author of this book did not, significantly, consider that a British work was worthy of inclusion in an account of the development of scientific sociology.

## Sociological theory

For a comprehensive account of the major schools of sociological theory and their historical development, the reader should consult Don Martindale, *The Nature and Types of Sociological Theory* (London, Routledge and Kegan Paul, 1961). An alternative is N. S. Timasheff, *Sociological Theory: Its Nature and Growth* (Rev. ed.; New York, Random House, 1964). A number of important issues are covered in John Rex, *Key Problems of Sociological Theory* (London, Routledge and Kegan Paul, 1963). For the philosophical and methodological issues raised in the process of theory-building, no better start could be made than reading Karl Popper, *The Poverty of Historicism* (London, Routledge and Kegan Paul, 1961). A good introduction to methodology in the social sciences and its relationship to theory is Maurice Duverger, *Introduction to the Social Sciences* (English trans.; London, Allen and Unwin, 1964). An approach to the analysis of social systems is contained in Kingsley Davis, *Human Society* (New York, Macmillan, 1964) and in George Homans, *The Human Group* (London, Routledge and Kegan Paul, 1962).

A statement of the essentials of the structural-functional approach is in Robert Merton, *Social Theory and Social Structure* (Rev. ed.; Glencoe, The Free Press, 1957), Chapter One 'Manifest and Latent Functions'. This book deserves a good deal of attention for it contains many important essays on sociological theory and its applications. Talcott Parsons is an influential but controversial figure whose work is difficult for the beginner in sociology. It is probably best to start with some of his *Essays in Sociological Theory* (Rev. ed.; Glencoe, The Free Press, 1954). For a critique of Parsons (and other sociologists) see C. Wright Mills, *The Sociological Imagination* (New York, Oxford University Press, 1959). A British criticism of Parsons is in an article by David Lockwood, 'Some Remarks on "The Social System"' (*Brit J. Sociology*, Vol. VII, No. 2, June, 1956). A full discussion of the conflict theory approach to society is in a book by the German sociologist Ralf Dahrendorf, *Class and Class Conflict in Industrial Society* (London, Routledge and Kegan Paul, 1959).

Discussions on role theory can be found in most of the major sociology textbooks, but especially in Johnson (1961) Chapters Two and Three. The British anthropologist Michael Banton is especially interested in the development of role theory, and his book *Roles* (London, Tavistock Publications, 1965) deserves attention. For an account of the various uses of the term 'role' the reader should consult the article by L. J. Neiman and J. W. Hughes, 'The Problem of the Concept of Role' in Stein and Cloward (1961). Apart from the application of role theory to social work contained in books such as Noel Timms, *Social Casework: Principles and Practice* (London, Routledge and Kegan Paul, 1964) and Helen Perlman, *Social Casework: A Problem-Solving Process* (Chicago University Press, 1957) there have been numerous articles in American social work journals. Among these are A. O. Foster, 'The Use of Social Science Concepts in the Diagnostic Process' (*Social Casework* Vol. XLIV, No. 7, July, 1963), a case example using role analysis, Dorothy Schroeder: 'Integrating Social Science Theory through Case Discussion' (*Social Casework*,

Vol. XLIV, No. 7, July, 1963), an account of the use of role and small group theory in case discussions in a family casework agency, and Max Siporin, 'The Concept of Social Types in Casework Theory and Practice' (*Social Casework* Vol. XLI, No. 5, May, 1960), on the use of the interpretation of informal social roles to clients.

## Family and culture

Studies on family structure and its relationship to the community have proliferated in Britain in recent years. The most well known have been those of the Institute of Community Studies, notably Michael Young and Peter Willmott, *Family and Kinship in East London* (London, Routledge and Kegan Paul, 1957), Peter Townsend, *The Family Life of Old People* (London, Routledge and Kegan Paul, 1957), Peter Willmott and Michael Young, *Family and Class in a London Suburb* (London, Routledge and Kegan Paul, 1960) and Peter Willmott, *The Evolution of a Community* (London, Routledge and Kegan Paul, 1963). These and other relevant British studies are all surveyed and evaluated in Josephine Klein, *Samples from English Cultures* (London, Routledge and Kegan Paul, 1965, Two Vols.). Attention should also be given to a recent study of family and kinship in a South Wales town, Colin Rosser and Christopher Harris, *The Family and Social Change* (London, Routledge and Kegan Paul, 1965).

A collection of over fifty articles, mainly American, are contained in N. W. Bell and E. F. Vogel, *A Modern Introduction to the Family* (London, Routledge and Kegan Paul, 1960). This is a most useful book for social workers, especially the articles in Parts III and IV on the internal processes of the family and the relationship between family and personality. Talcott Parsons and R. F. Bales, *Family, Socialisation and Interaction Process* (London,

Routledge and Kegan Paul, 1956) combined sociological analysis with psychoanalytic concepts in looking at personality development (see especially Chapter Two 'Family Structure and Socialisation of the Child'). Parsons and Ralph Linton contribute theoretical essays to the collection of articles edited by Ruth Ashen, *The Family: Its Function and Destiny* (Rev. ed.; New York, Harper, 1959) which includes studies of the family in different societies. An inexpensive paper-back in the 'Foundations of Modern Sociology Series' by William J. W. Goode, *The Family* (New Jersey, Prentice-Hall, 1964) covers in a systematic way the nature of family relationships. In the National Institute for Social Work Training Series Four is Eileen Younghusband (ed.), *Social Work with Families* (London, Allen and Unwin, 1965) which contains articles drawing substantially on sociological material. Social workers will be particularly interested in those family patterns which appear to contribute to deviant behaviour in parents or children. Apart from consulting the relevant sections in Bell and Vogel (1960) Parts III and IV and Smelser and Smelser (1963) Part III, reference should be made to Arnold Rose (Ed.), *Mental Health and Mental Disorder* (London, Routledge and Kegan Paul, 1956) a collection of articles which includes Marie Jahoda's 'Towards a Social Psychology of Mental Health', deserving special attention. One of the most challenging and influential recent books in this field is R. W. Laing and A. Esterson, *Sanity, Madness and the Family* Vol. One (London, Tavistock Publications, 1964). An important piece of research in this field by a social worker is E. M. Goldberg, *Family Influence and Psychosomatic Illness* (London, Tavistock Publications, 1958).

On the subject of class influences on behaviour, reference should be made first to general reading on social class. A substantial collection of articles is included in R. Bendix and S. M. Lipset (eds.), *Class, Status and Power* (London,

Routledge and Kegan Paul, 1958). Of particular interest in this book are Part I, 'Theories of Class Structure' and Part III, 'Differential Class Behaviour'. Section IV of Stein and Cloward (1961) covers social stratification, while Riessman, Cohen and Pearl (eds.), *Mental Health of the Poor* (Glencoe, The Free Press, 1964), deals with material of direct relevance to social work practice both within and outside psychiatric settings. There are a number of articles in American social work journals which may be consulted, including Shirley Hellenbrand, 'Client Value Orientations: Implications for Diagnosis and Treatment' (*Social Casework*, Vol. XLII, No. 4, April, 1961) and Florence Kluckhohn, 'Cultural Factors in Social Work Practice and Education' (*Social Service Review*, Vol. XXV, 1951).

## Social work organisation

One of the most valuable introductions to the study of organisations is P. M. Blau and R. W. Scott, *Formal Organizations* (London, Routledge and Kegan Paul, 1963) which, while covering a wide range of topics in organisational analysis, draws throughout for illustration on research studies made by the authors on social work agencies. Reference should also be made to P. M. Blau, *The Dynamics of Bureaucracy* (University of Chicago Press, 1955). Section VI, 'Bureaucratic Structure' in Stein and Cloward (1961) should be consulted and Amitai Etzioni, *Modern Organisations* (New Jersey, Prentice-Hall, 1964) provides a brief introduction to the whole field. Wilfred Brown and Elliot Jaques, *Glacier Project Papers* (London, Heineman, 1965) contains essays of primary interest to students of industrial organisation, but the first contribution by Wilfred Brown on 'Organisation and Science' looks at fundamental theoretical issues and deserves to be widely read.

Specifically related to social work and social administration are the collection of case studies by David Donnison and Valerie Chapman, *Social Policy and Administration* (London, Allen and Unwin, 1965). This book sketches a general theoretical framework for looking at the social services from an organisational point of view, and includes useful notes on the literature in the field. H. L. Wilensky and C. N. Lebeaux, *Industrial Society and Social Welfare* (New York, Russel Sage Foundation, 1958) is an account of the development of social work in the United States within a socio-cultural context, and Chapter Ten 'Agency Structure and Social Welfare Policy' is particularly relevent.

*The use of sociological knowledge*

There is little easily accessible literature on the problems associated with the application of sociological knowledge to social work practice. Noel Timms *Social Casework: Principles and Practice* (London, Routledge and Kegan Paul, 1964) refers to some of the problems, and A. J. Kahn (ed.) *Issues in American Social Work* (Columbia University Press, 1959) contains some useful contributions by A. Kadushin and J. W. Eaton. Another collection of articles, Cora Kasius, *New Directions in Social Work* (New York, Harper, 1954) includes A. J. Kahn on 'The Nature of Social Work Knowledge' and H. S. Maas and M. Wolins on 'Concepts and Methods in Social Work Research'. The following articles from American journals point to some of the issues involved in applying sociological knowledge to practice, namely Ernest Greenwood, 'Social Science and Social Work —A Theory of Their Relationship' (*Social Service Review*, Vol. XXIX, 1955), Otto Pollack, 'Exploring Collaboration between Casework and Social Science in Practice' (*Social Work Journal*, Vol. XXXIII, 1952), and Donald Young,

'Sociology and the Practising Professions' (*American Sociological Review*, Vol. XX, December, 1955).

On the problems of, and the opportunities for, research in social work see Norman Polansky (ed.), *Social Work Research* (University of Chicago Press, 1960) and the article by Ann Shyne: 'Case Work Research: Past and Present' (*Social Work* (U.K.) Vol. 21, No. 3, July, 1964). Particularly concerned with the application of sociological theory to social work research is the collection of articles edited by L. S. Kogan, *Social Science Theory and Social Work Research* (New York: National Association of Social Workers, 1960) which deals with general theoretical and methodological issues, and pays special attention to the research implications of role theory, organisation theory, and small group theory.

# Bibliography

ABERELE, D. F. and NAEGELE, K. D. (1952) 'Middle Class Fathers' Occupational Role and Attitudes Towards Children', *Amer. J. Orthopsych*, Vol. 52.

ADORNO, T. W. *et al.* (1950) *The Authoritiarian Pesonality*, New York: Harper.

ANDRESKI, S. (1964) *Elements of Comparative Sociology*, London: Weidenfeld and Nicolson.

ASHEN, R. (1959) ed. *The Family: Its Function and Destiny*, Rev. Ed. New York: Harper.

BANTON, M. (1964) 'Role', *New Society*, No. 84, 7 May.

BANTON, M. (1965) *Roles*, London: Tavistock Publications.

BARNES, H. E. and BECKER, H. (1938) *Social Thought from Lore to Science*, Vol. II, Boston.

BATESON, G. *et al.* (1956) 'Toward a Theory of Schizophrenia', *Behavioural Science*, Vol. 1, No. 4, October.

BELL, N. W. and VOGEL, E. F. (1960) eds. *A Modern Introduction to the Family*, London: Routledge and Kegan Paul.

BENDIX, R. and LIPSET, S. M. (1953) eds. *Class, Status and Power*, London: Routledge and Kegan Paul.

BERNSTEIN, B. (1960) 'Language and Social Class', *Brit. J. Sociology*, Vol. XI, No. 3, September.

BERNSTEIN, B. (1964) 'Social Class, Speech Systems and Psychotherapy', *Brit. J. Sociology*, Vol. XV, No. 1, March.

BERNSTEIN, B. (1965) 'A Socio-Linguistic Approach to Social Learning', *Penguin Survey of the Social Sciences*, Gould, J. (ed.), London: Penguin.

BLAU, P. M. (1955) *The Dynamics of Bureaucracy*, University of Chicago.

BLAU, P. M. and SCOTT, R. W. (1963) *Formal Organizations*, London: Routledge and Kegan Paul.

BOSSARD, J. H. S. and BOLL, E. S. (1960) *The Sociology of Child Development*, 3rd. Ed., New York: Harper.

BOTT, E. (1957) *Family and Social Network*, London: Tavistock Publications.

BOTTOMORE, T. B. (1962) *Sociology: A Guide to Problems and Literature*, London: Allen and Unwin.

BROWN, W. and JAQUES, E. (1965) *Glacier Project Papers*, London: Heinemann.

CAUDILL, W. (1958) *The Psychiatric Hospital as a Small Society*, Cambridge: Havard University Press.

CHINOY, E. (1955) *Automobile Workers and the American Dream*, New York: Doubleday.

CHINOY, E. (1964) *Society: An Introduction to Sociology*, New York: Random House.

COSER, L. (1956) *The Functions of Social Conflict*, London: Routledge and Kegan Paul.

DAHRENDORF, R. (1959) *Class and Class Conflict in Industrial Society*, London: Routledge and Kegan Paul.

DAVIS, A. (1950) *Social Class Influences on Learning*, Cambridge.

DAVIS, K. (1964) *Human Society*, New York: Macmillan.

DAVISON, E. (1965) *Social Casework*, London: Ballière.

DENNIS, N., HENRIQUES, F. and SLAUGHTER, C. (1956) *Coal is Our Life*, London: Eyre and Spottiswoode.

DEVEREUX, G. (1963) 'Two Types of Modal Personality Models', *Personality and Social Systems*, Smelser, N. J. and Smelser, W. T. (eds.) New York: Wiley.

DOLLARD, J. and MILLER, N. E. (1950) *Personality and Psychotherapy*, New York: McGraw-Hill.

DONNISON, D. and CHAPMAN, V. (1965) *Social Policy and Administration*, London: Allen and Unwin.

DURKHEIM, E. (1938) *The Rules of Sociological Method*, Eng. trans., Glencoe: The Free Press.

DURKHEIM, E. (1952) *Suicide: A Study in Sociology*, Eng. trans., London: Routledge and Kegan Paul.

DUVERGER, M. (1964) *Introduction to the Social Sciences*, Eng. trans., London: Allen and Unwin.

ETZIONI, A. (1964) *Modern Organization*, New Jersey: Prentice-Hall.

FARIS, R. E. L. and DUNHAM, W. H. (1939) *Mental Disorders in Urban Areas*, University of Chicago Press.

FLOUD, J. E., HALSEY, A. H. and MARTIN, F. M. (1956) *Social Class and Educational Opportunity*, London: Heinemann.

FOSTER, A. O. (1963) 'The Use of Social Science Concepts in the Diagnostic Process', *Social Casework*, Vol. XLIV, No. 7, July.

GARDNER, B. B. (1945) *Human Relations in Industry*, Chicago: Irwin.

G O L D B E R G, E. M. (1955) 'Some Developments in Professional Collaboration and Research in the U.S.A.', *Brit. J. Psych. Social Work*, Vol. III, No. 1.

G O L D B E R G, E. M. (1958) *Family Influences and Psychosomatic Illness*, London : Tavistock Publications.

G O L D T H O R P E, J. and L O C K W O O D, D. (1963) 'Affluence and the British Class Structure', *Sociological Review*, Vol. 11, No. 2.

G O L D T H O R P E, J. (1965) paper delivered at British Association. Summarised in *New Society*, No. 154, 9 Sept.

G O O D E, W. J. (1964) *The Family*, New Jersey : Prentice-Hall.

G O U L D N E R, A. W. (1957) 'Cosmopolitans and Locals', *Administrative Science Quarterly*, No. 2.

G O U L D N E R, A. W. (1964) 'Anti-Minotaur : The Myth of a Value-Free Sociology', *The New Sociology*, Horowitz, I. L. (ed.) New York : Oxford University Press.

G R E E N, A. (1958) 'The Middle Class Male Child and Neurosis', *Social Perspectives on Behaviour*, Stein, H. D. and Cloward, R. A., (eds.) Glencoe : The Free Press.

G R E E N W O O D, E. (1955) 'Social Science and Social Work : A Theory of their Relationship', *Social Service Review*, Vol. XXIX.

H A L S E Y, A. H., F L O U D, J. E. and A N D E R S O N, C. A. (1962) *Education, Economy and Society*, Glencoe : The Free Press.

H E L L E N B R A N D, S. C. (1961) 'Client Value Orientations : Implications for Diagnosis and Treatment', *Social Casework*, Vol. XLII, No. 4. April.

H O L L I N G S H E A D, A. B. and R E D L I C H, F. C. (1958) *Social Class and Mental Illness*, New York : Wiley.

H O L L I S, F. (1959) 'Contemporary Issues for Caseworkers'. Paper read at Smith College School of Social Work.

H O M A N S, G. C. (1962) *The Human Group*, London : Routledge and Kegan Paul.

H O W A R T H, E. *et al.* (1962) 'The Canford Families', *Sociological Review Monograph*, No. 6, Keele.

I N K E L E S, A. (1964) *What is Sociology?*, New Jersey : Prentice-Hall.

I R V I N E, E. E. (1956) 'Transference and Reality in the Casework Relationship', *Brit. J. Psych. Social Work*, Vol. III, No. 4.

J A C K S O N, B. and M A R S D E N, D. (1962) *Education and the Working Class*, London : Routledge and Kegan Paul.

K A D U S H I N, A. (1959) 'The Knowledge Base of Social Work', *Issues in American Social Work*, Kahn, A. J. ed. Columbia University Press.

K A H N, A. J. (1957) 'Sociology and Social Work : Challenge and Invitation', *Social Problems*, Vol. IV. No. 3, January.

K A R D I N E R, A. *et al.* (1945) *The Psychological Frontiers of Society*, New York : Columbia University Press.

K A S I U S, C. (1954) *New Directions in Social Work*, New York : Harper.

KAUFMAN, I., PECK, A. L. and TAGIURE, C. K. (1960) 'The Family Constellation and Overt Incestuous Relations between Father and Daughter', *A Modern Introduction to the Family*, Bell, N. W. and Vogel, E. F. (eds.) London: Routledge and Kegan Paul.

KERR, M. (1958) *The People of Ship Street*, London: Routledge and Kegan Paul.

KLEIN, J. (1965) *Samples from English Cultures*, Two Volumes, London: Routledge and Kegan Paul.

KLUCKHOHN, F. (1951) 'Cultural Factors in Social Work Practice and Education', *Social Service Review*, Vol. XXV.

KOBRIN, S. (1951) 'The Conflict of Values in Delinquency Areas', *Amer. Sociological Review*, Vol. XVI, October.

KOHN, M. (1959 a.) 'Social Class and Parental Values', *Amer. J. Sociology*, Vol. LXIV, January.

KOHN, M. (1959 b.) 'Social Class and the Exercise of Parental Authority', *Amer. Sociological Review*, Vol. XXIV, June.

KOHN, M. (1960) 'Social Class and the Allocation of Parental Responsibility', *Sociometry*, Vol. XXIII, December.

KOGAN, L. S. (1960) ed. *Social Science Theory and Social Work Research*, New York: National Association of Social Workers.

LAING, R. W. and ESTERSON, A. (1964) *Sanity, Madness and the Family*, Volume I: 'Families of Schizophrenics', London: Tavistock Publications.

LEONARD, P. T. (1963) 'Family Casework and the Child Guidance Clinic', *Social Work* (U.K.), Vol. 20, No. 2, April.

LEONARD, P. T. (1964) 'Depression and Family Failure', *Brit. J. Psych. Social Work*, Vol. VII, No. 4.

LEONARD, P. T. (1965) 'Social Control and Class Values in Social Work Practice', *Social Work* (U.K.), Vol. 22, No. 4, October.

LOCKWOOD, D. (1956) 'Some Remarks on "The Social System" ', *Brit. J. Sociology*, Vol. VII, No. 2, June.

LUTZ, W. A. (1964) 'Marital Incompatibility', *Social Work and Social Problems*, Cohen, N. A. (ed.), New York: National Association of Social Workers.

MADGE, J. (1963) *The Origins of Scientific Sociology*, London: Tavistock Publications.

MARSHALL, T. H. (1963) *Sociology at the Crossroads*, London: Heinemann.

MARTINDALE, D. (1961) *The Nature and Types of Sociological Theory*, London: Routledge and Kegan Paul.

MAUS, H. (1962) *A Short History of Sociology*, London: Routledge and Kegan Paul.

MAYO, E. (1949) *The Social Problems of an Industrial Civilization*, London: Routledge and Kegan Paul.

MAYS, J. B. (1962) *Education and the Urban Child*, Liverpool University Press.

MCIVER, R. M. (1931) *The Contribution of Sociology to Social Work*, New York: Columbia University Press.

MCKINLEY, D. G. (1964) *Social Class and Family Life*, Glencoe: The Free Press.

MERTON, R. T. (1957) *Social Theory and Social Structure*, Rev. Ed. Glencoe: The Free Press.

MEYER, C. H. (1959) 'The Quest for a Broader Base for Family Diagnosis', *Social Casework*, Vol. XL, No. 7, July.

MILLER, D. R. and SWANSON, G. E. (1960) *Inner Conflict and Defense*, New York: Holt.

MILLS, C. W. (1951) *White Collar*, New York: Oxford University Press.

MILLS, C. W. (1959) *The Sociological Imagination*, New York: Oxford University Press.

NEIMAN, L. J. and HUGHES, J. W. (1961) 'The Problem of the Concept of Role—A Re-Survey of the Literature', *Social Perspectives on Behaviour*, Stein, H. D. and Cloward, R. A., eds. Glencoe: The Free Press.

NURSTEN, J. (1964) 'Role Conflict in Adolescence', *Social Work* (U.K.), Vol. 21, No. 4, October.

NURSTEN, J. (1965) 'Social Work, Social Class and Speech Systems', *Social Work* (U.K.), Vol. 22, No. 4, October.

OLDS, V. (1962) 'Role Theory and Casework: A Review of the Literature', *Social Casework*, Vol. XLIII, No. 1, January.

PARSONS, T. (1937) *The Structure of Social Action*, New York: McGraw Hill.

PARSONS, T. (1952) *The Social System*, London: Routledge and Kegan Paul.

PARSONS, T. (1954) 'Psychoanalysis and Social Structure', *Essays in Sociological Theory*, Rev. ed. Glencoe: The Free Press.

PARSONS, T. and BALES, R. F. (1956) *Family, Socialization and Interaction Process*, London: Routledge and Kegan Paul.

PARSONS, T. and FOX, R. (1960) 'Illness, Therapy and the Modern American Family', *A Modern Introduction to the Family*, Bell, N. W. and Vogel, E. F. (eds.), London: Routledge and Kegan Paul.

PARSONS, T. (1963) 'Social Structure and the Development of Personality', *Personality and Social Systems*, Smelser, N. J. and Smelser, W. T. (eds.), New York: Wiley.

PERLMAN, H. H. (1957) *Social Casework: A Problem Solving Process*, Chicago University Press.

PERLMAN, H. H. (1960) 'Intake and some Role Considerations', *Social Casework*, Vol. XL, No. 4, April.

POLANSKY, N. (1960) *Social Work Research*, University of Chicago Press.

POLLACK, O. (1952) 'Exploring Collaboration between Casework and Social Science in Practice', *Social Work Journal* (U.S.), Vol. XXXIII.

POPPER, K. R. (1961) *The Poverty of Historicism*, London: Routledge and Kegan Paul.

REUSCH, J. (1953) 'Social Factors in Therapy', *Psychiatric Treatment*, 31., Wortis, S. B., Herman, M. and Hare, C. C. (eds.), Baltimore: Williams and Wilkins.

REX, J. (1963) *Key Problems in Sociological Theory*, London: Routledge and Kegan Paul.

RHYS WILLIAMS, T. (1959) 'The Personal-Cultural Equation in Social Work and Anthropology', *Social Casework*, Vol. XL, No. 2, February.

RICHMOND, M. (1917) *Social Diagnosis*, New York: Russell Sage Foundation. Reprinted 1955.

RIESMAN, D. (1958) *The Lonely Crowd*, New York: Doubleday. Abridged.

RIESMAN, D. and GLAZIER, N. (1952) *Faces in the Crowd*, Yale University Press.

RIESSMAN, F. (1962) *The Culturally Deprived Child*, New York: Harper.

RIESSMAN, F., COHEN, J., and PEARL, A. (1964) eds. *Mental Health of the Poor*, Glencoe: The Free Press.

ROBINSON, V. (1939) *A Changing Psychology in Social Work*, University of North Carolina Press.

ROETHLISBERGER, F. J. and DICKSON, W. J. (1939) *Management and the Worker*, Havard University Press.

ROSE, A. (1956) ed. *Mental Health and Mental Disorder*, London: Routledge and Kegan Paul.

ROSE, A. (1957) 'Theory for the Study of Social Problems', *Social Problems*, Vol. IV, No. 3, January.

ROSENBLATT, A. (1962) 'The Application of Role Concepts to the Intake Process', *Social Casework*, Vol. XLIII, No. 1, January.

ROSSER, C. and HARRIS, C. (1965) *The Family and Social Change*, London: Routledge and Kegan Paul.

SCHAFFER, L. and MYERS, J. K. (1959) 'Psychotherapy and Social Stratification', *Advances in Psychotherapy*, Cohen, M. B. (ed.), New York: Norton.

SCHROEDER, D. (1963) 'Integrating Social Science Theory Through Case Discussion, *Social Casework*, Vol. XLIV, No. 7, July.

SEARS, R. R., MACCOBY, E. E. and LEVIN, H. (1957) *Patterns of Child Rearing*, New York: Row Peterson.

SHYNE, A. (1964) 'Casework Research: Past and Present', *Social Work* (U.K.), Vol. 21, No. 3, July.

SIMEY, T. S. (1956) 'Social Research and Social Casework', *Boundaries of Casework*, Association of Psychiatric Social Workers.

S I M E Y, T. S. (1964) 'What is Truth in Sociology', *New Society*, No. 95, 23 July.

S I M O N, H. (1961) *Administrative Behaviour*, 2nd. Ed. New York: Macmillan.

S I P O R I N, M. (1960) 'The Concept of Social Types in Casework Theory and Practice', *Social Casework*, Vol. XLI, No. 5, May.

S M E L S E R, N. J. and S M E L S E R, W. T. (1963) eds. *Personality and Social Systems*, New York: Wiley.

S P I E G E L, J. P. (1960) 'The Resolution of Role Conflict within the Family', *A Modern Introduction to the Family*, Bell, N. W. and Vogel, E. F. (eds.), London: Routledge and Kegan Paul.

S P I N L E Y, B. M. (1953) *The Deprived and the Priveleged*, London: Routledge and Kegan Paul.

S T A N T O N, A. H. and S C H W A R T Z, M. S. (1954) *The Mental Hospital*, New York: Basic Books.

S T E I N, H. D. and C L O W A R D, R. A. (1961) eds. *Social Perspectives on Behaviour*, Glencoe: The Free Press.

T A Y L O R, F. W. (1911) *Scientific Management*, New York: Harper.

T A Y L O R, R. K. (1958) 'The Social Control Function in Casework', *Social Casework*, Vol. XXXIX, No. 1, January.

T I M A S H E F F, N. S. (1964) *Sociological Theory: Its Nature and Growth*, Rev. Ed. New York: Random House.

T I M M S, N. (1964 a.) *Social Casework: Principles and Practice*, London: Routledge and Kegan Paul.

T I M M S, N. (1964, b.) *Psychiatric Social Work in Great Britain 1939-1962*, London: Routledge and Kegan Paul.

T I T M U S S, R. M. (1954) 'The Administrative Setting of Social Service', *Case Conference*, Vol. 1, No. 1, May.

T I T M U S S, R. M. (1958) *Essays on 'The Welfare State'*, London: Allen and Unwin.

T O D D, P. H. (1961) 'Some Comparisons in the Development of English and American Casework', *Social Casework*, Vol. XLII, No. 8, October.

T Ö N N I E S, F. (1955) *Community and Association*, Eng. trans., London: Routledge and Kegan Paul.

T O W N S E N D, P. (1957) *The Family Life of Old People*, London: Routledge and Kegan Paul.

V O G E L, E. F. and B E L L, N. W. (1960) 'The Emotionally Disturbed Child as a Family Scapegoat', *A Modern Introduction to the Family*, Bell, N. W. and Vogel, E. F. (eds.), London: Routledge and Kegan Paul.

V O I L A N D, A. L. *et al.* (1962) *Family Casework Diagnosis*, New York: Columbia University Press.

V O L D, G. B. (1958) *Theoretical Criminology*, New York: Oxford University Press.

W A R D E L L, W. I. (1955) 'Social Integration, Bureaucratization, and the Professions', *Social Forces*, May.

WEBER, M. (1947) *The Theory of Social and Economic Organization*, Eng. trans., New York: Oxford University Press.

WEBER, M. (1958) *The Protestant Ethic and the Spirit of Capitalism*, Eng. trans., New York: Scribner's.

WEISMAN, I. and CHWAST, J. (1960) 'Control and Values in Social Work Treatment', *Social Casework*, Vol. XLI, No. 9, November.

WHYTE, W. H. (1959) *The Organization Man*, London: Cape.

WILENSKY, H. L. and LEBEAUX, C. N. (1958) 'Industrial Society and Social Welfare, New York: Russell Sage Foundation.

WILLMOTT, P. (1963) *The Evolution of a Community*, London: Routledge and Kegan Paul.

WILLMOTT, P. and YOUNG, M. (1960) *Family and Class in a London Suburb*, London: Routledge and Kegan Paul.

WINNICOTT, C. (1964) 'Casework and Agency Function', *Child Care and Social Work*, Codicote Press.

WOOTON, B. (1959) *Social Science and Social Pathology*, London: Allen and Unwin.

WRONG, D. H. (1961) 'The Oversocialized Conception of Man in Modern Sociology', *Amer. Sociological Review*, Vol. XXVI, April.

WYNNE, L. C. *et al.* (1958) 'Pseudo-Mutuality in the Family Relations of Schizophrenics', *Psychiatry*, Vol. XXI, May.

YOUNG, D. (1955) 'Sociology and the Practicing Professions', *Amer. Sociological Review*, Vol. XX, December.

YOUNG, M. and WILLMOTT, P. (1957) *Family and Kinship in East London*, London: Routledge and Kegan Paul.

YOUNGHUSBAND, E. (1965) ed. *Social Work with Families.* London: Allen and Unwin.